Giddy Up, Eunice

D0028393

CALGARY PUBLIC LIBRARY

DEC   2016

Giddy Up, Eunice

Because Women Need Each Other

SOPHIE HUDSON

author of the BooMama blog

B&H
PUBLISHING GROUP

NASHVILLE, TENNESSEE

Copyright © 2016 by Sophie Hudson
All rights reserved.
Printed in the United States of America

978-1-4336-4311-8

Published by B&H Publishing Group
Nashville, Tennessee

Author represented by Alive Literary Agency, 7680 Goddard Street, Suite 200, Colorado Springs, Colorado 80920, www.aliveliterary.com

Dewey Decimal Classification: 248.843
Subject Heading: WOMEN \ CHRISTIAN LIFE \ HUMAN RELATIONS

Unless otherwise noted, all Scripture is taken from the English Standard Version, (ESV) copyright © 2001 by Crossway Bibles, a publishing ministry of Good News Publishers. ESV Text Edition: 2007. All rights reserved.

Also used: Holman Christian Standard Bible (HCSB), copyright © 1999, 2000, 2002, 2003, 2009 by Holman Bible Publishers, Nashville, Tennessee. All rights reserved.

Also used: New Living Translation (NLT), copyright © 1996, 2004, 2015 by Tyndale House Foundation. Used by permission of Tyndale House Publishers Inc., Carol Stream, Illinois 60188. All rights reserved.

Also used: The Message (MSG), copyright © 1993, 1994, 1995, 1996, 2000, 2001, 2002 by Eugene H. Peterson.

Also used: The Amplified Bible (AMP), copyright © 2015 by The Lockman Foundation, La Habra, CA 90631. All rights reserved.

1 2 3 4 5 6 7 8 • 21 20 19 18 17 16

For Mama, who has always loved,
honored, and served so beautifully

Contents

Foreword

I love Sophie Hudson. I love the way she thinks. I love the way she relates. I love the way she writes. I love the way she loves. I have the privilege to know her on the back side of the page where every writer lives real life. Sometimes the sides of those pages don't match. I'm writing this foreword to let you know Sophie's pages are true, front and back.

She's in the thing. Life is what I mean. She's fully engaged and out there where the heart is vulnerable and the winds can blow hot or cold. She risks loving even if it means losing. Sophie is a servant in a serve yourself world. She is a teacher in every aspect of life and I suspect the root of her excellence is embedded in the soul of an insatiable student.

I like a lot of things about Sophie, but two top my list: she loves Jesus and she loves people. I don't mean that in the "don't we all?" sense. I mean really. She studies Jesus like "all the treasures of wisdom and knowledge are hidden in Him." (Col. 2:3) She studies people like each individual is a full-color anthology, bound up in a soft cover of human flesh.

There is a third thing I particularly like about Sophie. She is just plain hilarious. I could compile a list of quotables from simple texts I receive from her. You are going to have a blast with Sophie Hudson in this book. You're going to sit next to her and see life through her spectacular and beautiful and sometimes mischievous eyes. And here's the best part: you're going to like life a whole lot better when you finish this book. It won't be because it's gotten any easier. It will be because some people just make living on planet Earth a whole heck of a lot more bearable. That's Sophie.

Enjoy,

Beth Moore, Living Proof Ministries

Introduction: What We Have Here is a Hitch in Our Get-Along

I don't know if it'll make you feel any better, but I think I need to tell you that the book you're holding in your hands right now has, like, *super* Christian-y origins.

Oh, no kidding. It's just a hair shy of signing up for Bible drill and then participating in a choir contest featuring the hymns of John Wesley.

Because the idea for this book? The very first "a-ha" moment I had related to it?

I don't mean to brag, but it totally happened during my quiet time one morning when I was smack-dab in the middle of a Bible reading plan with my church.

Thank you. Thank you so much.

That's a pretty earnest start for a book, don't you think? I mean, it's not quite as good as if I'd been in my prayer closet (I don't really have a prayer closet) and memorizing the entire book of Leviticus (honestly, I have a hard time making it through Leviticus; that is a LOT of rules, y'all) while someone played

"Come, Ye Sinners, Poor and Needy" on a four-string banjo in the background.

But it worked in a pinch.

And while I will spare you the tale of how I fell off of the Bible reading plan bandwagon a couple of months later thanks to a big ole looming deadline, that quiet time moment has stayed with me for the last year and a half.

Perhaps I should explain.

On that particular day of the Bible reading plan, we were in Luke 1, which, you know, didn't necessarily seem like the most significant or exciting passage to be covering that morning. However, I fought the urge to resume my *Parenthood* marathon on Netflix and plowed ahead. For a whole host of reasons, I'm so glad I did.

Now you may know this next part already, but I'll go ahead and spell it out since I am the reigning queen of overexplaining. In Luke 1 we hear all about how Gabriel visited Zechariah with the news that his wife Elizabeth, who was "advanced in years," was going to have a baby who would be filled with the Holy Spirit even in the womb. Since we have the benefit of history, we know that baby was John the Baptist, but Zechariah didn't—which is why he openly doubted Gabriel and then had to deal with the unfortunate consequence of not being able to speak. That's a tricky thing for a priest.

Sure enough, Elizabeth turned up pregnant (that's the lesser-known Mississippi translation of the Bible). She "kept herself hidden" (Luke 1:24) for about five months (so would I, by the way, if I found out I was expecting in my sixties), but she was grateful for what the Lord had done.

Meanwhile, up in Nazareth, Gabriel paid another visit to a young woman named Mary. He informed her that she was going to have a child—the Savior of the world, no less—and after Gabriel finished with his big announcement, Mary responded with one of my favorite understatements ever:

How will this be, since I am a virgin? (Luke 1:34)

After Gabriel told her precisely how it would be, he gave her the sweetest news in verses 36–37:

And behold, your relative Elizabeth in her old age has also conceived a son, and this is the sixth month with her who was called barren. For nothing will be impossible with God.

When I read those two verses last February, I underlined and starred them with my purple pen, and I wrote myself this note at the top of the page:

"God gave Mary someone who would understand."

Think about it. Mary and Elizabeth's circumstances were oh-so-similar, but they were at vastly different stages in their lives. Two completely different generations. To put it in modern terms, Mary was super-excited because she just updated the apps on her iPhone, and Elizabeth was looking through her AARP magazine before she double-checked Zechariah's 401K account.

But as C. S. Lewis once said, "Friendship is born at that moment when one person says to another: 'What? You, too? I thought I was the only one.'"

That C. S. Lewis was a pretty smart fella.

I had no idea at the time, of course, but that February morning was just the beginning of my time with Mary and Elizabeth. In fact, they've been hanging out in my head ever since. And last fall, when I transitioned into a new job as Women's Advisor at a Christian high school where I'd previously worked as an English teacher for fourteen years, it dawned on me that there were Marys everywhere I turned. There were Marys at the lockers, Marys in the lunchroom, and Marys trying to plug in flat irons in my office because MY HAIR, MRS. HUDSON, DO YOU SEE HOW BAD MY BANGS LOOK? Granted, the specifics of their lives don't necessarily resemble those of Elizabeth's young cousin in Nazareth, but their need for support, affirmation, and confirmation in the midst of uncertainty?

Pretty much exactly the same.

And day after day, as they'd sit three deep on my tiny office sofa or stop by to stock up on tissues after an argument with a boyfriend or—I KID YOU NOT—walk in my office between classes to ask if I had "any of that chocolate that's, like, hard on the outside but kind of creamy on the inside because I am, like, SO CRAVING that texture," I'd think about their precious lives, so simple and so complex all at the same time, and I'd ask myself the same two questions over and over.

How in Sam Hill do we keep these girls connected and committed to the body of Christ?

Who are the older women who relate to them and encourage them and bless them like crazy?

4

Most of them have their mamas, of course. Praise the Lord for sweet mamas.

But I think we all know that there are gaps that mamas can't fill. I'm actually convinced that there are gaps that mamas aren't meant to fill.

And while you may not need for me to spell it out, I'll go ahead and say it anyway: these Millennial girls need us, y'all. They need us something awful. They may be a generation who can create a smoky eye with ease and snap selfies at angles that would send most of us to the orthopedic ward, but when it comes to walking in the confidence of their callings? Resting in the peace and assurance that they are deeply loved by their heavenly Father?

I'm not gonna lie. Sometimes they're a little shaky.

And here's what we all know: the younger girls aren't the only ones who are struggling.

Late last year I spoke at a conference in South Carolina. My session was on a Saturday afternoon, which means that, true to form, around 8:00 Friday night I was seized by what could only be described as a blazing, white-hot panic. I decided that my message was dumb, my stories were stupid, and it would probably be better for everybody if I ditched the whole thing and instead compiled some sort of comprehensive visual recap of the first four seasons of *The Real Housewives of Beverly Hills*.

Make no mistake, people. Reality television can teach us some lessons.

By 10:00, though, I'd resigned myself to proceeding with my original (dumb) talk in its original (stupid) state. It was about our good friends Mary and Elizabeth, and the gist was that we need to keep our spiritual eyes wide open as we walk our unique, God-ordained roads because (1) we need each other, and (2) sometimes the folks God sends to walk with us don't look anything like what we expect.

Well, really, that wasn't the entire message, but we'll talk about all of that later. In the meantime, I figure we can skip the bullet points and focus on the point of this particular story.

My Saturday afternoon session started right on schedule, and I was maybe thirty minutes into my talk when I mentioned something that occurred to me out of nowhere the night before: one of the perils of being an Elizabeth in our current culture is the danger of reaching "a certain age" and deciding that we're pretty much done with church. We get tired and we get burned out and we make up our mind that our Kingdom usefulness is over. Finished. Done.

And I was just about to move on to the next point when I realized that somewhere to the right of where I was standing, a woman was crying. Sobbing, really. I quickly looked over the tables at the front of the room until I spotted a lady with her face buried in her hands. Friends on either side reached out to comfort her, and as I choked out my next few sentences, I hoped that somewhere in the middle of her grief she could hear the words that the Lord impressed so clearly on my heart the night before:

"If you're in a place where you feel like your usefulness (to the body of Christ) is questionable, that is a lie. These women in this room need you. The women in your church need you. We need you. You stay in it."

The same goes for you, too, you know.
We need you.
You stay in it.

So it's just a hunch, but I'm guessing that right about now you may be thinking, *Um, I'm not trying to mind your business or anything, but the title on the front of this book says something about Eunice, and so far we've talked a whole lot about Mary and Elizabeth. I THINK THAT PERHAPS YOU'VE MADE AN ERROR.*

And I get it. I'd probably be thinking the same thing if I didn't have the benefit of a handy book outline sitting in front of me.

It turns out those verses from Luke 1 that so resonated with me a year and a half ago have stuck with me. They've led me to some unexpected places and some unexpected people in Scripture. In fact, there are several instances in Scripture where we see the life-changing, Kingdom-building impact of women from different generations who are working together, loving one another, and serving the body. We have our girls Mary and Elizabeth, for starters. Naomi and Ruth also come to mind. And then there's Lois and Eunice (some of you type-A folks just totally exhaled because FINALLY, THERE SHE IS), a grandmother/mother combo who poured their "sincere faith" into Timothy.

So for those of you keeping score at home, that gives us one pair who were navigating the unique terrain of their (unexpected) callings, one pair who were fighting their way through heartbreaking circumstances on the road to redemption, and another pair who were establishing a legacy of faith in their family.

I don't know about you, but I relate to every stinkin' one of them.

Ultimately, though, if we're splitting hairs, my location on the time line of generational similarities is probably closest to Eunice. As best we can tell, Eunice was middle-aged (I prefer to think of it as *in the prime of her life*, but that's just my personal perception), a regular ole mom who was doing her best to tag-team with her mama and teach her son about the things that really mattered.

Well.

Several months ago I was soaking up a rare moment of quiet in my office, and I found myself thinking about the Eunice-ness of this current stage of life. I do my best to take care of my little family, to work hard at my job, and to keep my house in a clean enough state that I'm not totally embarrassed if a neighbor pops over to visit or borrow an egg. I also like to try to find, you know, A MINUTE to hang out with my friends every once in a while, not to mention that tending to my inner introvert requires me to spend at least one evening a week wrapped up in a blanket while I watch Chip and Joanna Gaines / Guy Fieri / Jeff Probst encourage someone to remodel a house / brine some brisket / conquer an elimination challenge.

So I guess what I'm saying is that, like most of us, I'm not operating with a whole lot of margin in my life right now. On top of that, there's the crystal-clear reality that the Eunice stage of life isn't even a tiny bit glamorous. Based on my own personal experience, I'd say that it mostly involves (1) big piles of laundry, (2) way too many trips to Publix, (3) a growing certainty that I will never again feel "caught up," (4) practice jerseys, practice fields, ball fields, and ball games, and (5) hepta-tons of caffeine (side note: hepta-ton is a unit of measurement reserved exclusively for women who find themselves mired down in Eunice-ness).

So if you add up all of that stuff and consider all the pieces and parts of life that require managing and tending, it's easy to feel overwhelmed. That's precisely how I felt during those few moments of reflection in my office. Every day seems to come complete with an endless to-do list, and I don't know about y'all, but I get tired. Sometimes I even feel a little bit bone-weary, but I totally understand if that sounds a little too dramatic coming from someone who just confessed that she spends at least one night a week *wrapped up in a blanket.*

Bless.

But here's what I can say without a second's hesitation: no matter what begs for our attention, and regardless of whether we relate to Mary, Elizabeth, Naomi, Ruth, Eunice, or Lois, life is infinitely richer when people are our priority. The end. We can sidestep it all we want to, and we can fill up our days with stuff that doesn't really matter (I am speaking to my own personal tendency to, for instance, spend the better part of a Saturday morning combing three or seven stores for a specific kind of pillowcase), but there's no getting around how much women need each other. The heart of the gospel is relationship, and God has hard-wired each of us with a longing to be seen, to be loved, and to be known.

We have to keep first things first, of course, and make sure we have the Lord and our families at the top of our relational totem poles. I also think it's good to remember that this isn't something we have to force. After all, we don't see a model in Scripture where young women are roaming the streets and saying, "IS THERE AN OLDER STRANGER WHO WOULD LIKE TO SPEAK INTO MY LIFE?" In fact, in each of these three pairs of women, there's already a built-in cross-generational connection. That's important, because it reminds us that we don't necessarily have to take on anything new; we may just need to open our eyes and look around at the people in the places where we already are.

I mean, I can't promise that you're going to find a mentor while you're sitting at work in the sixteenth meeting of the week or sampling the latest delicacy from the frozen foods section of Costco, but stranger things have happened, you know?

And here's a huge thing to remember: we don't have to take on all the tasks and all the things and all the people at once. I remind myself of this about eleventy times a day. Just this morning I was trying to figure out where I can carve out some time for a few of my favorite college-aged friends, and the image of a square dance popped in my mind. At first I thought that was super odd, but after a few minutes the visual made sense to me: you stay in a circle, stay connected, stay facing forward—but you move around. You dance for a few minutes with one person, then you cross over and grab someone else's hand. Then you dance with that person a little while. And you keep on going until, eventually, you come back to where you started.

You're constantly moving—we can all relate to that—but you're also constantly connected. And even as you reach out to move forward, you're still reaching behind—all the while creating a pattern that works for everybody.

For whatever reason, that makes perfect sense to a Eunice like me.

One last thing before we dive into what I hope will be a deep and refreshing relationship pool. (And is it possible for time in a pool to be funny? Because I would love it if our time together could also be funny.)

(Please, Lord, let it be funny.)

There have been so many times in my life when I've gotten this whole cross-generational friendship thing so very, very wrong. In my twenties, for instance, I just wanted to be the cool older friend, and as a result I didn't teach my younger friends much of anything except how to survive a Friday at work if you had way too much to drink on Thursday night. I didn't have any appreciation for how closely those younger girls were watching me (and watching their other older friends, as well), so I didn't take my place in their lives nearly as seriously as I should have. That is why I can say with everything in me that living your life without any concern for how it affects the people behind you is like jumping on a fast track and traveling at breakneck speed to a very special place called THE LAND OF MISSED OPPORTUNITIES AND ALSO REGRETS.

Trust me when I tell you that you'll want to leave just as soon as you get there.

By the same token, there have been times in my life when I have been so dismissive of older, wiser voices that I'm flat-out ashamed. I could list example after example of bad decisions that

were born out of either an insistence that I knew better or a deter-
mination to prove someone else wrong.

Dumb, dumb, dumb.

But that's precisely why getting a little older can be so dadgum
redemptive.

And it's precisely why we don't need to waste a second of the
privilege.

Most of us, I think, want to love the people around us really
well. We would say that we want to be women of great faith,
women who pass on the "sincere faith" of 2 Timothy to the
younger people in our sphere of influence. We also want to be
women who learn from the Loises (and the Elizabeths) (and the
Naomis) in our lives.

So I say let's go.

Let's love each other and pour into each other and soak up wisdom from each other—and let's cross generational lines to do it.

Saddle up, sister.

This is going to be fun.

Mary and
Elizabeth

Chapter 1

Some Cousins and Some Babies and Some Callings

For the last couple of days I've been trying to remember what life was like when I was fourteen.

And what I can tell you without hesitation is this: fourteen was some deep awkward, y'all.

However, I was fairly clueless about the level of awkward I exhibited on a daily basis, so I was happy as could be.

I had great friends. I thought Jake from *Sixteen Candles* was, like, THE CUTEST. I loved my black pants that had suspenders attached to them because they looked awesome with a frilly white blouse and red flats. I read everything I could get my hands on, especially if Danielle Steele wrote it. I memorized funny movies. I realized that writing an essay in English class was instantly familiar. I memorized every word of Michael Jackson's *Thriller* album. I discovered that I loved having guy friends. I got my braces off. And most importantly at that point in my life, I made cheerleader.

Well, I was actually an alternate who got pulled off the bench when one of the girls on the squad moved out of town.

Nevertheless, I was so thrilled to get to be a part that I practically pledged my allegiance to Two Bits, toe-touches, and pom-pom routines when I showed up for my first practice.

And here's what strikes me when I look back on that time in my life: if I had a care in the world, I didn't know it. I faithfully went to school and dance and piano and youth group and Family Night Supper. My friend Melissa G. turned fifteen before everybody else, and along with her driver's license she received a sahweet brown Honda Accord hatchback, also known as our ticket to freedom. Melissa drove all of our girlfriends around on the weekends, and the reprieve from our parents' sedans made Saturday nights feel like the final dance scene in *Footloose*.

(Well, if *Footloose* had taken place at the Subway on 8th Street in my hometown.)

(And if it featured a supporting cast of ninth grade girls who thought the Spicy Italian sandwich was, like, the tastiest, fanciest food item ever because it was, like, SO NEW YORK CITY to eat salami in Mississippi.)

Even with all the unavoidable early-teenager awkward, I can honestly say that life at fourteen was, like, *totally major*. My friends and I experimented with blue mascara and frosted pink lipstick and told each other how pretty we looked. We teased our bangs to staggering new heights thanks to curling irons and Vidal Sassoon hairspray. We knew all the words to "Purple Rain" and "When Doves Cry" and sang both at the top of our lungs. And if we wanted to rock out, well, there were only two possible options: (1) "Born in the USA" with Bruce Springsteen, or (2) PETRA.

Church culture ran deep, y'all.

We lived, for the most part, in a bubble of unconditional love and acceptance. In the grand scheme of things, uncertainty and rejection were nowhere on our relational radar. I had no idea at the time, of course, but fourteen cemented my sense of being connected to the people around me. Fourteen gave me a down-to-the-marrow sense of belonging and security.

And while part of that came from my funny, smart, Spicy Italian sandwich-loving friends, here's what I see so clearly now: the primary people who passed along the gift of belonging were the older women in my life. Hands down. No question. It really didn't matter if they were a little older or a lot older; the point is that they looked out for me, encouraged me, taught me, listened to me, and blessed me. It almost felt like there was an endless reserve of people—Mama, Sister, my aunt Chox, my friends' mamas, my sister's friends, my teachers—who cared about my friends and me and wanted the absolute best for us.

And while yes, of course, everybody went through tough times and families struggled and life was by no means perfect, there was very much a mentality that we could—and should—help each other through just about anything.

We had wonderful men in our lives, too. Oh my goodness. I certainly don't want to diminish their enormous influence. But as a very young woman, the love and care and nurturing of older women taught me a lesson I didn't even know I was learning.

Everybody—no matter the age—craves a safe place with safe people.

It's a truth I absorbed as I moved from geometry class with Mrs. Carlisle, who patiently taught me as I struggled, to English class with Mrs. Reynolds, who continually pushed me as I soared. I picked up on it as I sat with my piano teacher and talked about way more than music, as I watched Sister come home on the weekends and sit on Mama's bed—or at Chox's kitchen table—for hours while they caught up on all the latest news. I tucked it deep in my heart, no doubt, when my older friends Ginger, Melinda, and Carah Lynn taught me the fine art of playing air drums to "Born to Run," when my friend Laura's mama would talk to us about God and grace and the blessing of community while we played round after round of Trivial Pursuit.

It's a pretty basic idea, right?

Nonetheless, it may very well be the very best gift that fourteen ever gave me.

And I've carried it with me ever since.

Since I have a job where I spend a big chunk of the school year listening to teenagers, I'm always on the lookout for resources that will "speak the kids' language" and "be real about issues" and "not sound too much like a lecture on bike safety from Mike Brady."

Well, a little over a year ago I was on the hunt for a resource about lust (no, really, it's fine—I feel like it's a good sign that we can talk about lust this early in our time together), and I ran across a sermon by Matt Chandler called "Freedom in the Fight."[1] For the record, it is one of the best sermons I've ever heard in terms of addressing the core issues behind lust and pornography, but feel free to totally exhale because I have zero intention of addressing those two topics.

However, there's most definitely something from that sermon that I want to talk about. It's a short verse from the book of Romans that Chandler (Matt? Rev. Chandler? Pastor Matt? Mandler?) references about five minutes in, and his countercultural application of the verse resonated like crazy with me:

> As we are his people and belong to him, God has asked us to interact in a certain way with one another. We are to care for one another, serve one another, and in fact outdo one another in honor, which means my head is always on a swivel looking to honor you, bless you, serve you, lower myself and exalt you for the sake of Christ, for the name of Christ every time I'm around you.[2]

Those are some pretty tall marching orders, don't you think? And since I didn't know if I'd ever really noticed that particular mandate in Scripture—that whole idea of outdoing one another in honor—I paused the sermon and hopped on the Google and looked it up.

Sure enough, I found the ESV translation of Romans 12:10: "Love one another with brotherly affection. Outdo one another in showing honor."

That verse rolled around in the back of my head as I listened to the rest of the message, and for the next week or so, I was tempted to do that self-righteous thing where I regarded the verse as something everybody else in the whole world needed to hear so that they could work out their personal issues.

For example.

I'll tell you what: somebody needs to tell Twitter about Romans 12:10.

Or.

Dear People in the Waiting Room Who Have Opted Not to Silence Your Phones: It is only my opinion, but I feel that a spirit of brotherly affection will be much more attainable when I can no longer hear you playing Candy Crush, hallelujah and amen.

And.

If I walk in this drugstore and the cashier screams "WELCOME TO WALGREENS!" I am going to turn around and tell him that his words do not in fact feel honoring to me because I AM AN INTROVERT and YELLING IS NOT VERY LOVING, SIR.

Eventually I started to think a little more deeply (and a lot less judge-y) about the words in Romans 12:10, and somewhere along the way, I discovered some insightful commentary from John Piper:

> The "one another" is not everybody, but fellow believers in the church. This doesn't mean you can't have affection for an unbeliever. You surely can. And it doesn't mean you shouldn't honor unbelievers. You surely should (1 Peter 2:7). But the focus here is on the church. Wherever else you have affection, have it here. And whomever else you honor, show honor here. So honoring means treating people better than they deserve.[3]

Piper (Most Rev. Piper? Brother John? JPipes?) goes on to say this:

> I think it boils down to "prefer to honor rather than be honored." If you try to out honor someone it means you love to honor more than you love to be honored. You enjoy

elevating others to honor more than you enjoy being elevated to honor. . . . Cultivate the love of honoring others.[4]

I think most of us would agree that all of this honoring and loving and elevating sounds very lovely and kind and generous. It's so great in theory, isn't it? That's why I couldn't help but wonder: *What does it look like*, really? *Where in Scripture do we see it in action? Who "[cultivates] the love of honoring others"?*

And yes, I know: JESUS. *Sure.*

PAUL. *Of course.*

But where else do we see people sincerely looking out for one another? Loving one another with brotherly affection? Where do we see folks outdoing one another in showing honor?

COLOR ME CURIOUS, Mandler and JPipes.

All of those questions ultimately reminded me of a passage I'd read in Luke 1 earlier in the year (remember when I mentioned that back in the intro?) (forgive me if I'm making your head spin with all of this thorough biblical scholarship) (*sarcasterisks*), and we're going to get to that in just a few minutes. Because I happen to think that Mary and Elizabeth had the whole "showing honor" thing down pat.

When it came to honor, those two were real pros.

Before we talk about Mary and Elizabeth, we need to make sure we're clear on how the Lord set the stage for Luke 1. So if you don't mind, let's travel back to 430 BC (-ish).

I'd encourage you to put on some comfy clothes, grab a light snack, and please, by all means, stay hydrated.

In the final book of the Old Testament, Malachi had a heart-to-heart with the people of Israel. They'd been back in the Promised Land for over a hundred years, and just like we've all been tempted to do in moments of perceived self-sufficiency, they got complacent. They turned to their own plans and their own interests and camped out in the wilderness again.

So, since God's people were bent on stubborn rebellion, they needed what my mama would call "a good talkin'-to." Maybe that's why the tone of this final book of the Old Testament almost feels like a family meeting; it was time to huddle up and STOP TALKING, KIDS, and listen carefully to what the Lord was saying. In this case the Lord opted to speak through His prophet Malachi, and His first words were tender and kind even though His children were way out of line:

"I have loved you," says the LORD. (Mal. 1:2)

That had to be sweet assurance, especially since the Israelites needed some significant course correction. God gently reminded them of His heart before He addressed the laundry list of offenses, and with His love for His people clearly established (this would be—what?—the 4,582nd time He'd told them?), Malachi moved through the improvement areas the Lord had identified: the priesthood, sacrifices, obedience, tithing, judgment, and repentance.

So basically Malachi covered some totally lighthearted topics in his first three chapters. And when he eventually neared the end of everything the Lord told him to say, he passed along a promise in chapter 4:

But for you who fear my name, the sun of righteousness shall rise with healing in its wings. You shall go out leaping like calves from the stall. (Mal. 4:2)

That's a pretty big promise—that "the sun of righteousness shall rise with healing in its wings"—but Malachi wasn't finished. In verses 5–6, Malachi closed the chapter with the Lord's assurance that there was one more significant somebody on the way:

Behold, I will send you Elijah the prophet before the great and awesome day of the LORD comes. And he will turn the hearts of fathers to their children and the hearts of children to their fathers, lest I come and strike the land with a decree of utter destruction.

At that point, to put it in modern terms, Malachi dropped the mic.

For the next four hundred years, no one heard a single word from the Lord or His prophets.

But the people of Israel never forgot God's promises.

And they waited.

Not having been alive during the Roman Empire, it's a little difficult for me to imagine what it was like to live in Israel around 6 BC. In those four-hundred-plus years since Malachi relayed God's prophecy to His people, the silence from the Lord must have been deafening. It must have been discouraging. And being fully in touch with my own impatience and strong sense of entitlement, it's pretty easy for me to imagine how frustrated and confused the Israelites must have been as they waited for the Messiah to appear. I can't help but think that if I had been around back then, hoping so desperately that the Lord would show Himself, I would have expected that whenever something finally happened, it was going to be big.

Huge.

GINORMOUS.

I mean, if Malachi had thrown down the whole "the sun of righteousness shall rise with healing in its wings" gauntlet, then I would be on the lookout for a spectacle. I would be thinking in terms of dark skies, parting clouds, trembling mountains, and whatever/whoever God promised arriving on the scene with some sort of dramatic soundtrack playing in the background.

Okay. I know. The Israelites didn't really have soundtracks. But I'd at least expect some trumpets. A few harps. A lyre or two.

But as it turned out, there wasn't even a tiny bit of fanfare. In fact, the first hint that God was up to something new? That the Messiah might very well be on the way?

An angel named Gabriel visited a priest named Zechariah in the quiet of the temple in Jerusalem. There was no pomp, no grandeur, and no sudden shift in the atmosphere that might fore-shadow something life-changing on the horizon.

There was just an angel (granted, that's kind of spectacular) and an old priest.

That's how God broke the silence and signaled that He was about to take up residence on earth.

So *flashy*, right?

The only reason Zechariah was even inside the temple that day was because his number came up (there were so many priests that they took turns going into the Holy Place to burn incense). He had served faithfully for years, and though he and his wife Elizabeth "were righteous in God's eyes, careful to obey all of the Lord's commandments. . . . They had no children because Elizabeth was unable to conceive, and they were both very old" (Luke 1:6–7 NLT).

And when Zechariah saw Gabriel at the altar, he was understandably terrified. I'll go ahead and wager a guess that he probably wasn't expecting a fertility update.

Sure enough, though, Gabriel told Zechariah that the Lord had heard his prayer, and Elizabeth was going to have a son named John, who "will be great in the eyes of the Lord" (1:15a NLT). Gabriel went on to say that John would be filled with the Holy Spirit before he was even born (that is fancy), and then he continued to let the prophetic punches fly:

> He will turn many Israelites to the Lord their God. He will be a man with the spirit and power of Elijah. He will prepare the people for the coming of the Lord. He will turn the hearts of the fathers to their children, and he will cause those who are rebellious to accept the wisdom of the godly. (1:16–17 NLT)

Can you even imagine? I'm sitting here thinking about how I hoped that our son, Alex, would smile by the time he was three months old and then maybe walk by his first birthday, and Zechariah got a rundown of his kid's destiny before Elizabeth was even pregnant. I mean, maybe I'm nineteen kinds of shallow, but

I'm pretty sure that if *all* I heard was that I was going to have a child who was filled with the Holy Spirit even in the womb, I'd jump on Twitter to share the news within three minutes and get the hashtag #LifeGoals trending in record time.

I'd also be tempted to post #BigDeal, #GodSaidSo, and #WorthTheWait, but that might be prideful.

Sure enough, Elizabeth got pregnant. Scripture tells us that she stayed inside for about five months. (I believe I've already established that if I ever experienced a pregnancy in my early sixties, I might not ever leave my house again.) Then, in Elizabeth's sixth month, Gabriel made another appearance; this time with a young girl in Nazareth named Mary.

And if the Israelites thought Elizabeth's pregnancy was unusual?

They hadn't seen anything yet.

I was thirty-two years old when I found out we were expecting our son.

I'd suspected as much for a few days. I'd been fighting off nausea and a general feeling of *ick* for over a week, but I'd kept my suspicions to myself and spent the better part of several days watching CMT and old episodes of *The Real World* while I sipped on ginger ale and picked apart sleeves of saltine crackers.

But by the fifth day of Nausea Fest, I was almost certain that there was a baby on the way. So around seven that night, when my husband David and I were in the middle of a discussion about, I don't know, something super important like *Alias* and Sydney

Bristow and all the reasons why I thought I might make a fine CIA operative, I offhandedly mentioned that *hey, here's some news, I think I might be pregnant.*

We were in the car and on the way to the drugstore within three minutes.

A half hour later, two little blue lines confirmed what I'd suspected for almost a week. David and I grinned nonstop for a solid forty-eight hours. We walked around in a haze of possibility and disbelief and excitement, knowing full well that our lives were going to change drastically but not having any way to anticipate how that change would look and feel.

But here's what occurs to me now: I was a pretty typical age for pregnancy. I was married. I had been to the doctor and told him I was ready. I had started prenatal vitamins and stocked up on folic acid. I knew full well that pregnancy was a very real and deeply desired possibility for me.

Even still, those two blue lines nearly bowled me over. As excited as we were, as much as we wanted that sweet baby, we were stunned to come face-to-face with the reality of it all. I don't want to oversimplify, but it occurs to me that the fresh awareness of new life almost always arrives with a little awe attached.

So when Gabriel appeared to Mary—who many scholars agree was somewhere around fourteen years old—well, I can only imagine her level of shock as he explained how the final piece of the prophecy from Malachi was going to fall into place. Gabriel didn't mince words, and the gist of what he said was this:

"Hey. So. You're gonna have a baby. He's going to be a little boy, and you will call Him Jesus. And the Lord will give Him David's throne so He can reign over the house of Jacob forever, and oh, by the way, His kingdom will have no end" (Luke 1:31–33, Sophie paraphrase).

I wouldn't blame Mary for one second if she stepped back and said, "UM, HAVE WE MET, STRANGER ANGEL?"

But to Mary's credit, she never doubted. She did ask a question, but that—at least in my opinion—just cements her spot at the top of the Biblical Understatement Tournament of Champions leaderboard. Because while there are lots of ways she could have responded when an angel showed up to tell her that she was going to give birth to the Son of God, I think "How will this be, since I am a virgin?" (Luke 1:34) showed some remarkable composure and restraint in the midst of great shock and surprise.

Even more impressive was that within minutes of hearing Gabriel's answer, Mary was all in with the Lord's plan. She said, "Behold, I am a servant of the Lord. Let it be to me according to your word" (1:38). No matter which way you look at it, her obedience is mind-boggling. She was a young girl, she was uneducated, she was poor, and she was from Nazareth. She was an unlikely candidate to be mother of the Savior of the world, and odds were that people would call her a liar—or crazy—if she shared any part of her conversation with Gabriel.

On top of all that, the Israelites were expecting the Messiah to arrive in some super-spectacular way, so Mary was destined, to a certain extent, to bump up against people's disappointments and doubts.

Nonetheless, she trusted Gabriel. She trusted the Lord. And when Gabriel told Mary that her cousin Elizabeth was also unexpectedly pregnant? Mary "arose and went with haste" to

Elizabeth's home seventy miles away in Judea. The trip was long and dangerous. But Mary didn't hesitate.

Can you imagine? She had to have been in a state. She was just minding her business, maybe thinking about her cute fiancé, and within a couple of minutes, Gabriel turned her whole world upside down. But Gabriel's news about Elizabeth meant that Mary wasn't nearly as alone in the whole visited-by-an-angel / unexpectedly expecting arena. SHE HAD A PERSON. She had a "Me, too."

And here's a big ole kicker: Mary's person just happened to be fifty years her senior.

Now doesn't that just make this situation all the more interesting?

When I think back on my life at fourteen from a present-day perspective, I realize oh-so-clearly just how sheltered I was. Unlike Mary, I was not at all acquainted with the phrase "earth-shattering," and the only thing that had really forced me out of my comfort zone was asking a boy to a summer dance that was sort of a rite of passage for the girls in my hometown.

I'm also well aware that if I had in fact been approached by an angel at that point in my life, I probably would have rolled my eyes and offered a quick reminder that, like, I really wanted to choreograph a new dance to "Wanna Be Startin' Somethin'," and he was, like, totally messing with my plans.

So it's probably safe to say that the majority of Mary's four-teen-year-old experience wouldn't have lined up with my own. I could not and cannot imagine the level of vulnerability and fear she must have experienced.

But there's one thing I think Mary and I both learned at fourteen, even if we learned it through completely different circumstances.

Everybody—no matter the age—craves a safe place with safe people.

And if we could build on that idea just a little bit, there's one more thing I want us to remember, because I think it's important.

We can find COMFORT and encouragement from someone in similar circumstances even if we don't belong to the same demographic.

It's so true, y'all. All too often, though, we look to the folks at our same age and stage and miss the wisdom and the perspective of someone who's a little farther along.

In Mary's case, that someone was named Elizabeth, and she was about seventy miles and fifty years down the literal and figurative road.

And while I certainly don't want to overpromise and underdeliver, I believe that the Lord can teach us so much through these two women. He wanted them walking through life together, and if we look closely, I think we can see some of the reasons why. In fact, I believe that we can identify some of what modern-day Christians are missing on the relational front if we look closely at how Mary and Elizabeth honored and cared for each other.

Because the provision that the Lord had in store for them?

The relational riches that were about seventy miles south of Nazareth?

Well, they were even better than Melissa G.'s Honda Accord hatchback that I mentioned earlier.

That, my friends, is saying something.

So for the next few chapters, we're going to hang out in Judea with Mary and Elizabeth. Their relationship can teach us a thing or nine—because funny things can happen when we open our eyes and our hearts and step outside our bubbles and oh, have mercy, our generations. We're going to look at how the Lord lined up their seemingly different paths, and we're going to see that despite the fact that they were in drastically different seasons of life, they were both on the verge of callings that would alter the course of human history.

We'll also take a few field trips to the Deep South—to Mississippi and Alabama and I want to say Georgia but the traffic is just terrible in Atlanta—and see how some of the lessons have played out in present-day life.

Feel free to play some dramatic soundtrack music at this juncture.

Trumpets, harps, lyres—and maybe a few banjos, too.

Chapter 2

Sort of Like The Odd Couple Except No One Was Named Felix

When I was a sophomore in college, I had a little bit of a come-apart over Homecoming.

And listen. In hindsight, I absolutely know that it wasn't a big deal at all. But there was a boy (of course) (almost every college come-apart was because of a boy) who I really hoped would ask me to be his date to the Homecoming football game and the parties that followed, and he asked someone else. I found out late one morning when I got back to my dorm room after class, and even though I played it cool and brushed it off and basically went through all the happy motions short of saying, "Look, everyone, at how unaffected I am," I knew by about 3 o'clock that afternoon that I was gonna have to get the heck out of Starkville before the emotional dam gave way.

So without telling a soul what I was doing or where I was going, I very discreetly grabbed my laundry bag, my purse, and my keys before I mustered every bit of my eighteen-year-old resolve and hurried down three flights of stairs to the basement parking lot. After I remembered where I'd parked, I threw my laundry bag on the passenger side, settled myself in the driver's seat, and cranked the car. I probably had to pull forward out of my parking space because I'm almost positive that was a time when my transmission was messed up and the whole "reverse" option wasn't being entirely cooperative, but that's really neither here nor there.

As soon as I turned onto the main road, I started to sob.

By that point, I think, the sobbing was 10 percent related to Homecoming, and 90 percent related to all my many, very deep feelings. It bummed me out that my nineteenth birthday was right around the corner because, like, MY TEENAGE YEARS ARE ALMOST OVER, Y'ALL. I felt sad that everybody seemed to have a boyfriend (or a prospective one) except for me. I was ticked that my major required me to take Early English Literature which, shockingly, listed exactly zero Flannery O'Connor or Eudora Welty or William Faulkner short stories on the syllabus because *BEOWULF,* for crying out loud. I lived in a perpetual state of dreading my botany class and inevitably gagged when I'd have to watch a movie in lab about a moth leaving its cocoon or a turtle laying eggs in the sand. And more than anything, I think, I missed being with Sister and my cousin Paige after spending the previous summer with them in Atlanta.

So, in summary, I was a hot mess: dateless, stressed, and headed home. I had a full-ish tank of gas, the *Stealing Home* soundtrack in the cassette player, and my laundry bag-riding shotgun.

(I mean, I was no fool.)

(If I was going to drive ninety emotionally charged miles to my parents' house, then I was going to at least get some clean clothes out of the deal.)

It was late afternoon when I finally turned down Mama and Daddy's driveway. I knew that Daddy was out of town, but Mama was home—and after I let myself in the back door, she met me coming around the corner by the laundry room.

"Sophie? What in the world? It's the middle of the week! What are you doing . . ."

And then she stopped—because within seconds of seeing my face, she somehow understood. In that way that is often unique to women, she intuitively knew that I was on the verge of falling apart. I didn't have to say a single word.

Mama hugged me, and I'll have you know that I didn't even cry; I'd left all my tears along that ninety-mile stretch of Highway 45. And for the rest of the evening, it was business as usual. Mama made us some supper, she asked what I thought about the way she'd rearranged the living room, and she told me all about a party her friend Edna had recently hosted. After an hour or so I decided to call my roommate, Daphne, to let her know where I was, and in the breeziest way imaginable, I told her I'd spontaneously decided that it would be fun to spend a night at home.

There's not a doubt in my mind that Daph knew what was up. But she let me have my version of things, and I hung up the phone knowing that I'd probably overreacted but feeling secretly relieved that my pride was mostly intact.

Through every single bit of whatever internal drama I had going on, Mama never pressed for information. She asked one question—"Are you okay?"—and when she was satisfied that I really was, that was it. While I'm sure she would have listened if I had filled her in on the details, getting the lowdown really wasn't her primary concern. I was.

Mama has always been super-intuitive and discerning, so I bet if someone had asked her the specifics of what was wrong with me, she would have come up with a pretty accurate assessment. In fact, she would have figured out which boy started the emotional tidal wave within three guesses (if she didn't already know the second she saw my face). But for those few hours I hung out at my childhood home on that fine September night, she set aside her maternal need-to-know (which I now recognize was NO SMALL FEAT), and she encouraged, she affirmed, she tended, and she blessed.

When I drove back to school early the next morning, my perspective was radically different. More than I needed someone to fix everything for me, I needed a safe place. And Mama's wisdom and care met me right in the center of that need.

I've never forgotten it.

Also, you'll be relieved to know that after I got a hold of myself and drove back to Starkville, someone did in fact ask me to Homecoming.

Just wanted to bring that around full circle for y'all.

There are only a few times in my life (including Homecoming-gate, of course) when I remember going somewhere "with haste"— you know, like when Mary travels to Elizabeth's house in Luke 1.

But I'll go ahead and admit that at least one of those probably involved some Popeye's fried chicken.

I'm not trying to say that the fried chicken is super-spiritual or anything. I am merely pointing out that there has been a time or eight in my life when I have experienced a fried chicken craving so strong that it might be better described as a *yearning*.

Normally, though, if I've gone somewhere "with haste"—if I've felt a sense of legitimate urgency—it was because of a relational connection. Sometimes it was because a loved one was hurting. Other times it was because I needed advice from a trusted friend. Or maybe it was because I just wanted to be with my mama.

So I think it's interesting that after Gabriel left her, Mary "arose and went with haste." That's the first thing she did. She got up, and she got going.

Specifically, she got going about seventy miles to the south, to her cousin Elizabeth's house in Judea. And since Mary didn't own a burgundy Buick Regal that had lost its ability to operate in reverse, she did what most women would have done at the time: she walked.

By most accounts the journey took her three or four days. And while I understand that it would be unfair to impose today's mentality about travel on Mary and her particular set of circumstances, I would just like to point out that if you ever hear that I walked seventy miles to see a cousin, you can be assured of this: I MUST HAVE BEEN DESPERATE FOR SOME COMPANY.

Nonetheless, walking long distances would have been fairly common for Mary, though I do think the fact that she embarked on such a long journey "with haste" gives us some insight into Mary's state of mind.

Let me see if I can break this down.

Mary was in a little bit of a cultural pickle. She was fourteen, she was unmarried, and she had just found out that she was going to give birth to, you know, the Savior of the world. But Gabriel made a point to relay the info that Mary's cousin, Elizabeth, was also pregnant, and Mary no doubt knew what an unexpected pregnancy that was since Elizabeth was about thirty years older than the average woman who signs up for the baby registry at Target.

From that perspective, the fact that Mary set out to see Elizabeth "with haste" makes perfect sense. If she had stayed in Nazareth, Mary would have been signing up for self-imposed isolation at best and social ostracism at worst. She knew the reality of life in her hometown, and she no doubt craved the companionship of her pregnant cousin in Judea.

There must have been something in Mary that didn't want to be alone.

There must have been some pondering about Elizabeth and Zechariah's situation.

And my guess is that after comparing options in Nazareth to options in Judea, there must have been a point when Mary thought, *I WANT TO GO TO THERE.*

So that's exactly what she did.

She walked seventy-plus miles over the course of three-plus days, which leads me to think she was a living, breathing heap of vulnerability when she finally "entered the house of Zechariah and greeted Elizabeth" (Luke 1:40).

One more hunch: That fifty-year age difference between her and Elizabeth? I'd be willing to bet that it was probably the very last thing on her mind.

When I think about all of that, here's what occurs to me.

It's so easy for people to feel like an inconvenience.

And don't get me wrong. I love me some people. But life gets busy and our schedules get packed and, if you're like I am, you can start to crave pajama time. Maybe even a little reality TV time. Because heaven knows that when real life is swirling all around, few things can get my mind off of a to-do list like the antics of a bunch of grown women who have opted to broadcast their lives to the masses via Bravo.

But when Mary showed up at Elizabeth's house, Elizabeth didn't treat her like an interruption. She didn't hide in a back room or roll her eyes or say that she would normally be so glad to talk but, um, she was SUPER busy watching the season finale of *The Real Housewives of Hebron*.

Instead Elizabeth was instantly and completely available to her young cousin. Scripture states that "when Elizabeth heard the greeting of Mary, the baby leaped in her womb. And Elizabeth was filled with the Holy Spirit" (Luke 1:41).

And lest we glance right over it, it's good to remember that "filled with the Holy Spirit" business. It was a whole new deal. In fact, Mary Elizabeth Baxter, who wrote Bible commentary in the late-nineteenth and early-twentieth centuries, pointed out that Elizabeth was the "very first person of whom such is mentioned."[5]

And it wasn't just that Elizabeth was the first person Scripture mentioned as being filled with the Holy Spirit; she also *reacted* and *responded* to Mary based on the knowledge the Holy Spirit gave her. In Luke 1:42, Elizabeth "exclaimed with a loud cry, 'Blessed are you among women, and blessed is the fruit of your womb!'"

In that moment Elizabeth knew a whole lot of information that no person shared with her, and she wasn't timid about it, either. Elizabeth's boldness—her "loud cry"—lets us know that she spoke with conviction and authority over her young cousin. She blessed Mary, she blessed the baby that Mary was carrying, and the only possible way she could have known to do either was because the Holy Spirit told her.

So Mary, after her long, arduous journey, was met with instant understanding. What a relief that must have been! According to Matthew Henry, "It does not appear that Elisabeth had been told any thing of her cousin Mary's being designed for the mother of the Messiah; and therefore what knowledge she appears to have had of it must have come by a *revelation*, which would be a great encouragement to Mary" (commentary, Luke 1:39–56).[6]

And I love this observation: "Mary had held no communication with Elizabeth. There was no penny post in those days. But the Spirit of God in one woman [recognized] the Spirit of God in the other, and it was a message from on high to Mary when Elizabeth [recognized] her as the Messiah's mother."[7]

Isn't that the neatest thing? When the Holy Spirit in me recognizes the Holy Spirit in you?

When we "get" what's going on without anyone telling us?

We need to pay attention to that. We need to *tend* to that. There is comfort and understanding in that place, and if I am ever tempted to discount it, all I have to do is think back on what a difference my very own mama made when she understood the High Drama of Homecoming without me having to give her a long-winded explanation.

That's such a tiny example, I know. Nowhere close to the mother of John the Baptist confirming the pregnancy of the mother of Jesus. But sometimes what we consider intuition is really wisdom and discernment given to us by the Holy Spirit. And whether we're talking about minor news or a major development, here's what has occurred to me over the course of studying this particular part of Mary and Elizabeth's story:

WHEN THE HOLY SPIRIT in one WOMAN RECOGNIZES and RESPONDS TO THE HOLY SPIRIT in ANOTHER WOMAN, SAFE PLACES BECOME SACRED SPACES.

And to be clear, I'm not talking about some big, touchy-feely moment where women get together and surf a wave of manufactured emotion.

But when we know we're in a sacred space, there's freedom to share our real lives and our real circumstances. To sincerely pray for one another. To bless each other. To listen with our hearts as well as our ears.

And that kind of freedom?

Oh my goodness. You'd better believe it can (and will) change some things. All too often in our relationships, however, we content ourselves with the superficial and miss the significant.

And we're selling ourselves short.

So, nobody asked me, but I'm going to tell you one of my very favorite things about God.

Ready?

One of my very favorite things about God is how He faithfully appoints people to walk with us at every single stage of our journey here on earth. And I don't mean that in any sort of *Bachelor*-y way, either. I just mean that people need other people, and throughout

Scripture we see a model of God providing people with friends and champions and mentors who support them and challenge them and spur them on.

He does the very same thing for us.

But let's be clear: *It may not look like we think it should.*

For example.

When I was a senior in high school, if you had asked me who I thought would be the very best person to walk with me on the road of my teenage life, I would have looked you straight in the eyes and maybe even yelled my answer.

Amy Grant.

AMY LEE GRANT.

Oh, yes ma'am.

Amy was everything wondrous to me when I was seventeen years old. In addition to the fact that she was a brilliant singer-songwriter, she seemed like she'd be that friend who was a little bit older but infinitely wiser, like she'd be able to quote a verse of Scripture for any situation, like she'd know all the best ways to tight-roll acid-washed jeans so that they looked their very best with Tretorns.

(Remember, it was the late '80s.)

(Acid-washed jeans wisdom was no small thing, my friends.)

And come to think of it, I would still like for Amy Grant to walk with me through some things. The years have done nothing to diminish my affection for her, and now that I'm a little older I might even be able to resist the urge to touch her face while humming "El Shaddai."

So far, though, the Lord has not seen fit to connect Amy and me even though I am borderline certain that it is His will for my life. He has, however, provided me with other wonderful people to walk alongside me, and it really is perfectly fine that not a single one of them has ever written and performed the beloved '90s classic "Baby Baby." They bring other things to the relational table.

Based on that, I'm guessing that if we had the ability to ask Mary who she wanted to walk with her through the whole immaculate conception / pregnant-with-Jesus situation, she probably wouldn't have listed her sixty-something cousin Elizabeth as her first choice. But just look how the Lord lined up their circumstances:

ELIZABETH	MARY
Elizabeth was unexpectedly, miraculously pregnant.	Mary was unexpectedly, miraculously pregnant.
Elizabeth's husband was visited by an angel.	Mary was visited by that same angel.
Elizabeth's baby was supposed to be very special, "filled with the Holy Spirit even in the womb."	Mary's baby was going to be, like, the Special-est baby in the history of the world.

Both women were in situations they never could have imagined.

And both women were on the verge of the callings of their lives.

Mary Elizabeth Baxter wrote, "What the communion of spirit between these two women was, and what the intense nearness to God, in the impossibility of explaining their position to man, it would be impossible to imagine. All unworthy in themselves, but wondrously privileged by God, the mother of the Messiah and the mother of His forerunner understood Him, and understood one another."[8]

I mean, can we all agree at this point that the Lord intended for the two of them to walk through their pregnancies together? Can we accept that if the Lord had wanted for Mary's same-age friends to be the ones to bless and confirm her pregnancy, He'd have found a way to get Mary to, I don't know, the Nazareth Mall?

Mary and Elizabeth were close to fifty years apart, but they didn't seem to get hung up on their differences. Mary didn't roll her eyes and say, *OHMYGAH, I can't go to Elizabeth's house; she's old enough to be my grandmother.* By the same token, Elizabeth didn't say, *No way am I hanging out with Mary; people under forty sort of get on my nerves.*

They trusted what they saw. They trusted what they knew.

And it makes me wonder: are our spiritual eyes wide open as we look for our people?

Or are we so programmed with a "same age, same stage" mentality that we're missing the women who are ahead of us and behind us?

And let me be clear: it's great to have friends who are about the same age. It's flat-out therapeutic to be able to discuss the day-to-day with people who are walking through the same stuff. To my way of thinking, this is not an either/or deal. It's a both/and.

We need people of all ages in our lives who will listen, encourage, and pray. We need people we can call and say, "Well, I think I've decided to quit church forever," or "Did you ever think that the only thing standing between you and certain divorce was a kitchen remodel?" or "Hey—when your kids were in junior high, did you ever worry that they were going to grow a third eyeball

and literally turn green before they climbed back into the space-
ship with the rest of the hormonal aliens?"

That last example is purely hypothetical.

We need each other so much, y'all.

And we are fools—FOOLS, I TELL YOU—if we think our
same-age silos are getting the relational job done.

I think Mary would probably agree.

Okay. Before we close out this chapter, we are going to have
a quiz.

I know. I didn't warn you. But it's just a pop quiz, and if it
affects your overall average in a negative way, then you will probably be able to talk me into some extra credit work because I am
kind of a pushover. Deal?

All righty.

Do you remember that sentence from earlier in the chapter
about safe places becoming sacred spaces?

Maybe?

Kinda?

No?

Well, since this is only a pop quiz, I will be so happy to remind
you because PUSHOVER.

Here it is.

WHEN THE HOLY SPIRIT in one WOMAN
RECOGNIZES and RESPONDS TO THE HOLY SPIRIT
in ANOTHER WOMAN, SAFE PLACES BECOME
SACRED SPACES.

And now that we've established a cross-generational component by digging a little deeper into Mary and Elizabeth's story, I want to take that idea one step further. Because apparently I have really strong feelings about this next thing:

In our current church culture, younger women and older women are desperate to walk through sacred spaces together.

I see it all the time when I go into churches to speak: younger women on one side of the room, older women on the other, both groups trying to figure each other out. I hear it, too. Younger women mention offhandedly that they don't have any family in town and they'd really like to have an older woman in their life. Older women tell me that they wish they knew how to connect with the younger girls—that it would be so fun to go to lunch or go shopping together—but it's like they're speaking different languages.

So there's definitely a desire to walk together, but unfortunately, for a whole host of reasons, we're (mostly) missing each other along the way. The good news, though, is that we can do this thing differently.

Mary and Elizabeth give us so much hope in that regard.

Chapter 3
I Do Not Understand You and Your Tricky Side Buns

I was four years old when *People* magazine made its debut.

I didn't read it, of course. I'm not entirely sure that I was reading anything back in those days, even if Mama vows and declares that I could identify every single word in *The United Methodist Hymnal* by the time I was three.

Apparently the combination of hymns and responsive readings made quite the impression.

Not to mention the overly optimistic lens of revisionist maternal history.

But when I was around seven, I fell headfirst into *People* magazine's grip. I will never forget riding to Atlanta in my aunt's station wagon, sitting on the wayback seat with my cousin Paige and flipping through the pages of an issue of *People* that my aunt Chox picked up at the Winn-Dixie earlier that day. The women from *Charlie's Angels* were on the cover (Kelly, Sabrina, and Kris, in case you're keeping score at home), and I was absolutely fascinated that

I could read articles about the people who played the characters I loved to watch on TV.

(This is probably about the time when you're thinking, *Um, you were SEVEN—what in the world were you doing watching Charlie's Angels?*)

(So it's probably a good time to remind you that I was the youngest child by ten years. My parents were in their mid-forties and putting their other two kids through college; my guess is that high-level supervision of my TV viewing wasn't at the tip-top of their priorities.)

(I feel like that's a safe assumption considering that just a few years later, we spent many meaningful Friday nights gathered 'round the TV for *Dallas*.)

That *People* magazine turned out to be the beginning of what would prove to be an, um, *significant* preoccupation with pop culture news. Even as a second grader (sweet mercy), I got a huge kick out of being able to peek behind the proverbial celebrity curtain. It was just all so glamorous and fascinating and a world away from my life in Mississippi.

So, from the time I was seven until I was about ten, I'd read Chox's and Sister's old issues of *People* and mentally file away whatever tidbits I read about Olivia Newton-John or Robert Redford or Diane Keaton. When I hit the preteen years, I moved on to *Tiger Beat* and *Teen Beat* because, um, RICK SPRINGFIELD, and after I started driving, I'd head straight for Brown's News Stand on Wednesday afternoons and stock up on my weekly magazine reading: *People, Us Weekly, TV Guide,* and maybe even a *Rolling Stone* for good measure. Between my magazine reading, my movie watching, and my habitual *Saturday Night Live / Late Night with*

David Letterman viewing, I was pretty much any Trivial Pursuit player's worst nightmare. I earned my varsity letter in pop culture nerdery, and I could sing all the words to the *Moonlighting* theme song if I needed to prove it.

("We'll walk by night / we'll fly by day / Moonlighting strangers / who just met on the way.")

(You're welcome.)

Pop culture didn't loosen its grip during my college years. I certainly don't mean to brag, but I was a charter subscriber to *Entertainment Weekly* and would sometimes read up on the backstory of the latest Kevin Costner movie when I was pretending to pay attention in philosophy class. Reading *EW* was my second-favorite alternate activity when I found myself in a boring lecture situation, but my preference was always to hide my friend Daphne's GameBoy behind a textbook and play Tetris to my heart's content.

I like to think that my discreet Tetris tactics were a forerunner to today's surreptitious classroom texting / Instagramming / FaceSnapTimeBooking, so you're welcome for that, Millennials. Maybe one day we can exchange fist bumps as a show of alternate activity solidarity.

By the time I got my first real job, I was as well-versed in the nuances of Dave Matthews Band / Hootie & the Blowfish / The Complete Film Catalog of Julia Roberts / Quotable Quotes from *SNL* as any twenty-three-year-old would hope to be. Throw in a fairly solid appreciation for country music, R&B, Academy Award trivia, and obscure TV shows of the '80s, and you can probably understand why I harbored a secret dream of competing on *Jeopardy*—provided that nothing related to math and/or science entered the question pool.

Listen. Everybody has gifts. Solving equations has never been one of mine.

There was, however, one completely unexpected reward for my years of overanalyzing *Beverly Hills 90210* and committing far too many song lyrics to memory: I could bond with teenagers within minutes, and this was no small feat as a first-year teacher. I might not have had a very, um, *solid* grasp of my subject area, but by diggity I could talk about Nirvana and Boyz II Men and *Pulp Fiction* and *Designing Women*. And somewhere in the mix of all those seemingly unrelated things, those kids and I found that there was more than enough room for all of us to stand on our relatively small patch of common ground.

For the next seven or eight years I continued to hold my own in the pop culture department; I somehow incorporated tidbits about Puff Daddy and Britney Spears and *Friends* and "Jenny from the Block" into my lessons at school, and I may have even admitted that I could rap the entirety of Will Smith's incomparable classic "Boom! Shake the Room."

(True story: I still know every word.)

("The rhyme is a football, y'all, and I went and threw it.")

When I was in my early thirties, though, something started to shift. I don't think I could have pinpointed exactly what it was, but I found that I related more to the middle-aged folks on *Survivor* than I did to the early-twenties crowd on MTV. I stopped watching the Grammys because I recognized fewer and fewer artists, and I unintentionally cut my movie-watching in half after I realized that I really enjoyed working in the yard. Then I got pregnant, and I had a baby, and I replaced *People* magazine with parenting blogs and Baby Einstein and VeggieTales.

And suddenly, one day when I was teaching tenth grade English, I knew that I'd reached the end of an era. I was helping kids with essay rough drafts, and one of my students had written a paper about his favorite bands. I skimmed over the first two body paragraphs, both about bands I knew, and as I started to read the third body paragraph, which was all about a band I had never heard of, I asked a question I'll never forget:

"So, do you think you need a better transition in this paragraph about Oar?"

Crickets.

I looked around to see if I'd missed some big classroom development, and eventually it dawned on me that my students were experiencing some degree of pity for me.

"What? What is it?" I asked.

"No big deal, Mrs. Hudson," the paper writer replied. "It's just that the band is O.A.R. You say the letters. OH. AY. ARE."

Listen. I know that it's silly. But I was so sad, y'all. I was embarrassed. Even though the music / TV / movie stuff was a strange connection to share with the kids I taught, it was still a connection, and not knowing the name of a pretty popular band signaled that I was way more at home with Nick Jr. than I was with MTV.

My failure to know O.A.R. meant that my pop culture dominance had reached its E.N.D.

And I'll tell you something else: I felt O.L.D.

Now I certainly can't speak to Nazareth's pop culture scene back in Mary's day, but who knows? Maybe there was a guy in

Mary's village who played a smokin' hot lyre and made all the girls' hearts beat a little faster when he'd let his hair fall in his eyes. Or maybe one of Joseph's buddies played in a harp ensemble called The Nazartastics. (I'm sorry. That's such a lame name. It's the best I can do considering that I am currently unfamiliar with any possible Nazareth High School mascots.) Or maybe Mary and her girlfriends liked to make up worship songs, and they'd sing them to each other as they walked behind their parents on the way to the temple.

Obviously I just made up all of those examples off the top of my head. But my point is this: teenagers typically find ways to separate themselves from their elders, and those of us who aren't teenagers are typically trying to find a way to play catch-up. Even in this last year I've felt some degree of pride that I was able to commit a solid 75 percent of Taylor Swift's *1989* album to memory, but as soon as I reached that milestone I realized that I'm still completely incapable of distinguishing all the different actors named Chris (Chris Pratt, Chris Pine, Chris Evans, Chris Hemsworth, Chris McGillicuddy, etc., and so on).

(As far as I know, Chris McGillicuddy is a completely pretend actor, but how could anyone possibly know that because MY WORD, THERE SURE ARE A LOT OF CHRISES.)

So I think it's safe to say that trying to keep up with the younger generation will wear you slap out. And fortunately, while their music and movies and TV shows are great connection points, they're not essentials. That's why, when I look at the story of Mary and Elizabeth, I find the sweetest relief in how they loved and responded to each other, because mercifully—thankfully—they didn't seem to get too hung up on all the different items and issues that might, under normal circumstances, constitute a generation gap.

In fact, we don't see a single indication that they were caught up in their generational differences. Elizabeth didn't roll her eyes because Mary was sporting a side bun. Mary didn't tell Elizabeth that her house was on fleek while Elizabeth wondered what in the world "on fleek" even meant. Elizabeth wasn't preoccupied with watching reruns of *Murder, She Wrote*, and Mary wasn't exasperated because her older cousin couldn't quote large chunks of dialogue from *Gossip Girl*.

From the onset of Mary's arrival, Elizabeth was all in with her much younger cousin. And from my perspective, at least, it seems like she was well aware that when the Holy Spirit gives you compassion for someone, it really doesn't matter how many years stand between your respective dates of birth. All that matters is responding to the prompting of the Holy Spirit and recognizing that any opportunity to speak into someone's life, bless them, pray for them, or minister to them—well, it is a privilege.

A PRIVILEGE.

Sometimes, though, we miss out on the privilege because we're so busy majoring on the minors. It's easy to feel like we won't "connect" because a few decades separate us, but we can absolutely trust the Lord to bridge the gap. It seems like Elizabeth knew that all too well; just look at her words in Luke 1:43–44:

> And why is this granted to me that the mother of my Lord should come to me? For behold, when the sound of your greeting came to my ears, the baby in my womb leaped for joy.

She didn't roll her eyes. She didn't comment on Mary's skirt length. She didn't launch into a lengthy monologue about how Mary's generation didn't understand the value of hard work and how, when she was a girl, she would have been able to make that walk from Nazareth to Judea in, like, HALF A DAY.

She welcomed Mary with open arms. She blessed Mary's pregnancy. And she rejoiced with her.

She rejoiced with her.

Sixteen years ago my husband and I moved to Birmingham. We knew a grand total of zero people here, but we knew that this is where the Lord wanted us. So we packed our stuff into a moving van and wondered all the while what it would be like to live in a city where we didn't know a soul.

You can appreciate that we arrived in Birmingham with just a tiny bit of trepidation. Because CITY FULL OF STRANGERS.

It was just a few weeks after we arrived when the wife of the man who hired me for my new teaching job called and asked if I'd like to be part of a Bunco group she was hosting. Back in the early 2000s we were all crazy for some Bunco, and I thought it sounded like a fun way to meet some folks. By that point I'd managed to make three new friends—Anna, Alison, and Norma Kay—and since they were also going to be part of the group, I felt like I might be on my way to finding my Birmingham people.

Thankfully, I was right about that.

And there was one other significant Bunco bonus.

Her name was Mary Jo.

Mary Jo was the person who invited me to be part of the group, and I liked her instantly. A mama of three grown children, she was somehow gracious and no-nonsense all at the same time. And since she was also a Mississippi native, we figured out pretty quickly that we shared a fondness for fried chicken, pine trees, and magnolias. The fact that she owned a fine assortment of brown transferware (that's a specific kind of china for those of you who do not consider dishes a worthwhile hobby) and had a knack for finding funky, comfortable shoes only elevated her in my personal estimation. She was most definitely someone I'd like to be if or when I finally grew up.

Our Bunco group lasted for three or four years before it transitioned into a Bible study (AS YOU DO). By that point I was in choir and Bible study at our church, so I'd catch up with Mary Jo over the occasional lunch or get-together. However, several years later—about the time that our son, Alex, started four-year-old kindergarten—I recognized that I was registering somewhere between desperate and cuckoo crazypants in terms of needing wisdom and counsel from older women. My mother and mother-in-law were both living in my hometown and quick to help whenever I asked, but I craved regular, face-to-face contact with women who had a few more years of wife-ing and mother-ing under their belts. None of the Bible studies at church worked with my schedule, so when it dawned on me that Mary Jo was still hosting a Bible study in her home on Wednesday nights, I knew that was my answer.

Also, I'm pretty sure I was about twenty minutes early the first week I attended, because does the phrase "AT WIT'S END" mean anything to you at all?

As it turned out, my friend Alison and I were the youngest people in our Bible study, and it was one of the best things that ever happened to me. The other women were in their forties, fifties, and sixties—in different stages of parenting and marriage and work than we were—and while I would often walk into Mary Jo's house filled with all manner of worries and questions and frustrations, I quickly learned to listen way more than I talked. I noticed over and over again that the ladies' conversations were consistently encouraging and edifying, full of affection and honor for their families and friends. They didn't pretend like life was perfect, so I didn't feel like I had to pretend, either, but there was an overarching tone of gratitude and joy that permeated our time together. If you've ever been part of what might be classified as a dysfunctional small group, you know what a relief it is to realize that the phrase "Bible study" doesn't have to be synonymous with "gossip and gripe session."

And those times when I did speak up? When I had a question about parenting a four-year-old or handling a relational conflict or stepping into something new with my writing? When I was feeling run down by the mama-guilt that frequently plagued me or facing a challenge I didn't think I could meet? Mary Jo and the other ladies always seemed to know exactly what to say. I doubt that they'll ever fully know how deeply they blessed me with their wisdom, their compassion, and their prayers.

We never made any official declaration of mentorship, but that's exactly what those women did in my life. That's exactly what Mary Jo still does. And imagine this: even though we don't necessarily share the same pop culture vocabulary, the Holy Spirit has managed to knit our hearts together just fine.

The fact that Mary Jo makes really good homemade cakes has only strengthened our bond.

Sometimes the Lord just goes above and beyond, doesn't He?

Now I don't want to overstep my boundaries, so bear with me—but it has occurred to me that there's something we don't see when Mary arrived at Elizabeth's house, and that something is anything resembling the following conversation:

"Elizabeth, I'm walking through some uncertainty right now. I'm unsure of how to move forward, and I would really value your insight into my current situation. Elizabeth, I come to you in all humility, and I have a question that I would be honored for you to consider. Would you mentor me?"

People of faith, we LOVE that question.

People of faith, I'm afraid that we can FREAK EACH OTHER OUT when we ask it.

I'm dead serious.

Over the last few years of writing and speaking, I've heard a significant number of stories from women who long to be mentored and can't find a single person in their community/church/workplace willing to step into that role. My heart absolutely goes out to folks who crave the guidance and care of an older woman; not being able to find it has to be discouraging and disconcerting and a whole bunch of other dis- words.

And make no mistake: mentoring is essential for healthy community. But part of the problem, I think, is that we may be asking the wrong question when we approach someone about mentoring us. It's a language that—for better or worse—many churches don't speak any more, and as a result of that, many *women* don't speak it, either. We hear the word "mentor" and we think of someone who has to be able to lead another woman through the Bible from Genesis to Revelation and show her how to maximize her budget and maybe even teach her to crochet while communicating the top ten most important aspects of holiness. There's some degree of misconception that a mentor is responsible for teaching us all there is to know about being a woman of God, and in my experience that puts a whole lot of pressure on both the mentor and the mentee.

Provided, of course, that "mentee" is actually a word.

But here's the good news: we can look to Mary and Elizabeth for some relief from the places where our expectations are unrealistic or maybe even unfounded.

First of all, this:

THERE ARE SOME MIGHTY FINE POTENTIAL
MENTORS WHO ARE ALREADY IN OUR LIVES
EITHER AS RELATIVES OR GOOD FRIENDS.

And if you're thinking, *No, that's not true—I don't even know any older people*, then I would like to take this opportunity to encourage you to invite a few from your church to lunch. Or coffee. Or bowling.

Well, maybe not bowling. We certainly don't want people throwing out their backs.

Regardless, here's what occurs to me: Mary doesn't seem to harbor any reservations about making the trek to Elizabeth's house, and that may well be because she already had a relationship with her. If that was the case, then there was already an established level of comfort, which may be why Elizabeth had a voice with Mary from the get-go. I personally think it's easier for a relationship with a mentor to take off long-term if there's already a friendship in place—or at least that's been my personal experience.

Secondly:

What we have in common far exceeds any perceived generational differences.

It's so easy to look at the generation behind us or the generation ahead of us and think that we just flat-out look at life differently. We can be tempted to get up on our generational high horses and think, *Well, I am unsure why these young Millennials seem to have leggings confused with pants. Leggings are not even a little bit able to serve in a pants-like capacity. What do these girls have against buttons and zippers?*

Or, those of us who might be a little too dependent on technology might think, *I am not really interested in having a mentor if she refuses to text, tweet, and Instagram. I can't live in a world where I might have to dial someone's phone number and talk on an actual phone, for crying out loud.*

However, Mary and Elizabeth remind us that when the Holy Spirit summons us to care for each other, generational differences fly out the window. The security of being loved and understood far outweighs any perceived advantage of having a mentor who can give you lots of hearts during a Periscope broadcast.

Just for the record, though: texting *is* pretty handy.

I promise I'm smiling.

Third thing:

> AT every AGE and STAGE oF LiFe,
> women need OTHeR women WHO wiLL
> LiSTen, ConFiRM, TeACH, bLeSS, and PRAY.

If nothing else, Mary and Elizabeth should remind us that women need each other—and when culture or circumstances or maybe cynicism threatens to keep us distant even though we are made for discipleship, we have to work that much harder to find our way into each other's lives. Maybe that means we seek out an older cousin. Maybe that means we turn around to the college girl who sits behind us every Sunday and invite her to lunch. Maybe that means a few of you thirty-somethings decide to spend a semester in one of your church's book clubs for the sixty-plus set.

(This may actually be one of my favorite ideas ever.)

(If you decide to do this, you have to e-mail me and tell me ALL ABOUT IT.)

Bottom line: we need each other, so we have to reach across the generations and find each other. And while nobody asked me, I think maybe the very best way to find a mentor is to first find a friend. When we're genuinely drawn to each other—when we share a genuine affinity for one another—friendship develops naturally and organically no matter the age difference.

And in lots of cases, those older friends will become mentors without anyone having to make a speech or a plea or an awkward ask. That being said, sometimes we know that the Lord wants us to go out of our way and make a speech or a plea or an awkward ask for mentorship from someone we don't know very well. If that's the case, then don't hesitate to be obedient to that prompting.

But however we form relationships with older and younger women, we can trust that intentionally stepping across generational lines is oh-so worth it. Because once we find our Mary or our Elizabeth (or both!), every aspect of our lives—our faith, our families, our careers, our friendships—will be all the better for it.

So the other day I was in my office at work, and two of my senior girls stopped by to say hey and visit for a few minutes. We talked about what they'd packed for lunch, what tests they had that week, and eventually they mentioned that they were super-excited about a concert that was coming up in a couple of days.

"OH!" I exclaimed. "Which concert?" As a general rule I still adore music, even if I don't listen to much of what the kids like.

(Well, except for T. Swift, of course.)

(Only I can't call her "T. Swift" in front of the girls at school because it creates cringe-inducing, please-Mrs. Hudson-we-beg-you-not-to-speak-our-lingo moments.)

The two seniors explained that they were going to see an R&B singer whose music I've never heard, but I've seen his name in the headlines way too many times. The look on my face must have conveyed my total lack of enthusiasm, and they said, "What? What is it, Mrs. Hudson?"

I stepped right up on my aforementioned old person high horse before I answered way too forcefully.

"I DO NOT THINK HE HOLDS A VERY HIGH VIEW OF WOMEN," I said—in a tone that might have been more appropriate reading the Declaration of Independence or some other Official Government Document.

I watched their faces fall thanks to my successful concert buzz kill, and I immediately felt super-convicted that I was pushing them away instead of drawing them in. I mean, if I want to have a voice in their lives, if I want to be able to bless and pray and teach and all those things I mentioned a few paragraphs ago, then I have to be aware that sometimes it's beneficial to muzzle a few of my opinions.

Heaven knows that even if I muzzle even half of them, I'll still have a lifetime's worth in my back pocket.

So I looked at the girls, smiled, and changed my tune.

"Look," I said. "His music is not for me. Clearly. After all, I'm 109 years old. But I hope y'all have fun. And when you come back to school next Monday, I want to hear all about it."

The girls' eyes lit up, and as they turned to leave, one of them looked back and said, "Sounds great, Mrs. H! We'll give you a full report!"

They were about two steps from the door when I jumped out of my chair to share one last encouraging word.

"HE REALLY DOESN'T SEEM TO RESPECT WOMEN, THOUGH!" I shouted way too cheerfully.

The girls laughed.

And obviously I still have a whole lot to learn about this mentor business.

But fortunately, thanks to Elizabeth and Mary Jo and the other older women in my life, I can count on learning lessons—especially about the stuff that really matters—from some really exceptional teachers.

However, I don't think they can teach me much at all about O.A.R.

That's why *People* magazine is still a mighty good resource in a pinch.

Chapter 4

Don't Worry, Kids—There's Room Enough for Everybody

I don't know if you know this about me or not, but I sort of enjoy watching television.

My affection for it is so great, in fact, that I would consider it a hobby.

Rest assured, though, that I don't think everybody needs to love it like I do. In fact, please do continue with your rock climbing and your gardening and your other outdoors-y pursuits. Know that I bless your efforts. And know that I will continue to bless those efforts while I am gearing up for a *House Hunters* marathon. After I warm up with a few episodes from season four of *Friday Night Lights* (I BELIEVE IN YOU, TIM RIGGINS).

So yes, I realize that it probably makes me seem shallow, but watching TV is one of my very favorite ways to relax. There are certainly other things I enjoy—cooking, writing, decorating, screaming my fool head off at college sporting events, etc.—but TV signals relaxation to me like few other activities do.

Please don't let that last sentence make you sad. I promise that the beach—in real, live nature—is the most relaxing place of all to me. However, if I could sit on the beach while watching television, I would probably lull myself into some sort of prolonged state of leisure that would render time meaningless and maybe even reverse the aging process. If I figure out a way to make that happen, then naturally you'll be the first to know.

And believe it or not, I actually have some great memories from my, um, FORTY YEARS of enthusiastic TV viewing. For example, way back when I was a little girl in the 1970s, if Tim Conway and Harvey Korman performed in a skit together on *The Carol Burnett Show*, one of them would inevitably start laughing before the skit was over. If any of the girls on *Charlie's Angels* needed to go undercover, they either wore a hat or a pair of glasses. (Kris was slightly more versatile; she'd braid her hair in pigtails and then speak with a Southern accent.) And whenever the family would watch a new episode of *Columbo*, my mama would usually fan her face and say, "*Whew*—I sure am glad I don't have to be in the room with him and that nasty cigar."

Mama has always had a very sensitive sense of smell.

When I was eleven or twelve, though, I noticed that TV started to change, and it wasn't just because I was getting older and becoming more aware of the dynamics between characters. Shows like *Dallas*, *Dynasty*, *Knots Landing*, and *Falcon Crest* had huge ratings (yes I watched them all, because, as I already mentioned, BABY OF THE FAMILY), and those shows ushered in a trend that's still with us today: Mean Girl TV.

Seriously. Female characters became increasingly angry, increasingly catty, increasingly manipulative—and increasingly mean to each other. The first I remember of it was Kristen and Sue Ellen on *Dallas*, and then Krystle and Alexis had an all-out cat-fight (in their silk blouses with shoulder pads, no less) on *Dynasty* while Mama and I sat slack-jawed in front of the TV, utterly astonished by the sight of (fictional) grown women treating each other that way.

And this was long before Krystle threw Alexis in the lily pond behind Carrington Manor, by the way, so I would not necessarily say that their relationship improved over time.

We had no idea way back then, but those shows were just the beginning of watching women exchange verbal and physical jabs. Yes, there were plenty of examples of women being supportive and encouraging, but meanness got way more attention. Then TV talk shows hit the mainstream, and while many of them featured legiti-mate human interest stories, a few seemed consistently bent on stirring up conflict to the point that women would lunge at each other. Scripted TV shows like *Melrose Place* continued the trend, and eventually reality television entered the fray.

In 2002, *The Bachelor* premiered, something I would consider a cultural game-changer. I can't think of another instance when TV producers put women in direct, weeks-long competition with each other for the affection of a man. That's why, in my opin-ion, *The Bachelor* signaled that all bets for civility were off. The metaphorical gloves were off, too. Because, if I may paraphrase the late-'90s hip-hop legend Coolio: "Ain't no catty like some *Bachelor* girls' catty 'cause the *Bachelor* girls' catty don't stop."

And please hear me: I'm not talking about all of this from some lofty, holier-than-thou tower. I think I've established that I LOVE ME SOME TV. I've watched all of these shows. I've even blogged about them. I thought I broke up with *The Bachelor* a couple of years ago, but apparently, thanks to this current season, we are most definitely "on" again. I can tell you that Bravo is channel 1181 in our cable system, and I can list every single one of the *Real Housewives* franchises. To a certain extent, I guess, I'm fascinated by how terrible women can be to each other because it's mercifully foreign to me. I've never been in a fight, I've never had a falling out with another girl, and I've never had someone verbally pummel me with a stream of expletives—which, by the way, WOULD BE A ROCK-SOLID CLUE THAT SOMEONE WAS NOT IN FACT MY FRIEND.

So, given that current culture isn't terribly supportive or instructive in terms of healthy relationships between women—and given a pervasive mentality that somehow more for me means less for you and more for you means less for me—how do we know what healthy, life-giving friendship looks like between two women?

You probably won't be surprised if I tell you that there's a pretty good example in Luke 1.

Because Elizabeth and Mary? They knew a better way.

I recognize that this is a bit of an understatement, but Elizabeth waited a long time to get pregnant. And whether we've personally struggled with difficulty conceiving a child or not, we can at least imagine how shocked Elizabeth must have been when she found out that she was finally going to have a baby.

In her sixties.

That's a bit of a curve ball, you know?

Obviously most women during Elizabeth's time started their families much earlier than we typically do now, so it wouldn't have been outside the realm of possibility for Elizabeth to have already been a great-great grandmother once she hit her sixties. Instead, though, God saw fit to make her a first-time mama on a *slightly* delayed schedule, and my guess is that she soaked up every second of the wonder of her pregnancy.

In fact, since we know that Elizabeth "kept herself in seclusion for five months" (v. 24 HCSB), it stands to reason that she was keenly aware of the physical and emotional changes that accompany pregnancy. Some uninterrupted time at home will do that for a person, you know. Plus, waiting for a child to arrive brings its own brand of expectancy—something that goes way beyond the anticipation of motherhood—and for that reason I imagine those five months must have been unsettling and surreal and extraordinary. After her initial realization that yes, she was going to have a child, there was the progression from morning sickness to a baby bump to baby flutters to baby kicks and baby flips.

I know it didn't *actually* happen, but it wouldn't have surprised me a bit if there were a verse tucked away in Luke 1 where Elizabeth stroked her growing belly and said, oh-so-sweetly, "THIS. IS. AWESOME."

The promise of new life always is.

So when Mary showed up at Elizabeth's house, Elizabeth was about two-thirds of the way through her own gloriously unexpected pregnancy. And I can't help but think that by modern standards—or at the very least by modern television standards—Elizabeth had every reason in the world to be TICKED OFF.

Seriously.

After all, she'd waited all of her adult life to be pregnant—she had wanted a baby for *decades*—and before she even had a chance to give birth, her young whippersnapper of a cousin showed up at her door, and she was pregnant, too.

I can't help think that if this whole scenario were to play out on television—or, you know, just in real life right now—there might be a moment where Elizabeth looks at Mary, rolls her eyes, and says, "Hey. Can I maybe just have A MINUTE to enjoy this pregnancy thing and feel, I don't know, SPECIAL? Because here I am, IN MY SIXTIES, feeling like a miracle because I'm finally having a baby, and then you walk up here all *BOOM. JESUS. SAVIOR OF THE WORLD?* That's a well-played trump card, sister. Good thing I enjoyed the spotlight before you snatched it right off of me."

Fortunately, though, Elizabeth set a way higher standard for people in general and women in particular. Because after she rejoiced with Mary in verse 42, she said the sweetest thing in verse 44: "For behold, when the sound of your greeting came to my ears, the baby in my womb leaped for joy."

Do you see that? It's not just Elizabeth that's over-the-moon excited for Mary; we also know that her baby—John, the forerunner of Jesus, the one who was filled with the Holy Spirit even in the womb—celebrated Mary's news, too.

And just as John no doubt kicked in Elizabeth's womb, here's the kick in our twenty-first-century pants: Elizabeth didn't feel competitive with Mary, she didn't think that more for Mary meant less for her, she didn't get down in the dumps because while yes, she was finally pregnant with a baby who Gabriel said would be very special, Mary got to be Jesus' mama, of all things.

Maybe Elizabeth was just super-selfless. Maybe she lived free from the pettiness and competition that binds up so many of us these days. Or maybe—just maybe—Elizabeth's contentment and confidence in her own calling left her feeling free to, as my mama would say, bless the fire out of her young cousin.

Elizabeth was FOR Mary. She didn't seem to feel like Mary was stealing her thunder; she didn't roll her eyes because she finally got her mama moment, and along came a teenage cousin who one-upped her. Elizabeth *could have* compared in that moment, because as excited as she was to be pregnant, Mary was pregnant with THE SAVIOR OF THE WORLD.

Elizabeth wasn't having any of that, though. She honored and rejoiced. She confirmed and blessed. Comparison and competition weren't anywhere on her radar.

Really, if you think about it, why would she react any differently? Why *wouldn't* she be thrilled to pieces?

And why are we not equally elated to see our sisters in Christ walk out whatever the Lord has called them to do?

Seriously—what is up with our imagined (and meaningless) competitions? Why do we wear ourselves out with comparison? Why do we create hierarchies in our heads? Why the generation gaps? Why do we tend so passionately to the ground surrounding our same-age, same-stage ministry silos?

What on earth?

We should be cheering for each other. Slapping each other on the back (gently, my friends—GENTLY). Encouraging each other to run hard and finish strong.

All too often, though, we're giving each other the side-eye. Calling out one another on social media under the guise of "concern." Making pointed comments about how someone better be careful that she doesn't get too big for her ministry britches.

We're made for more than that, y'all.

And by the grace of our very good God, we can do better.

Last year singer / songwriter / entertainer extraordinaire Taylor Swift (though I think I've made it clear that I like to refer to her as T. Swift when I'm in the privacy of my home) went on a massive world tour. I don't know the exact figures, but I think she had upwards of two hundred people at EVERY. SINGLE. SHOW.

Okay. Maybe it was more like fifty thousand.

And make no mistake: Tay-Tay (my second favorite nickname) is legit, y'all. Over one million people saw her *1989* concert tour (real talk: I totally got that info from Wikipedia, so GRAIN-O-SALT, my friends), and while I personally have not seen her in concert, by all accounts she puts on a phenomenal show.

Well, one recurring bit on the *1989* tour was that Tay-Tay brought out a group of her friends to "walk the runway" when she'd perform her hit song "Style." That rotating crew of musicians, models, actors, and other awesome folks became known as Taylor's "squad." Naturally, then, #squad became a favorite for group pictures on Instagram, though we probably need to acknowledge that if I, a forty-something mama, am writing about it, the #squad trend has more than likely begun its cultural descent. I am still going to talk about it, though, because I think it points to something bigger in terms of our girls Mary and Elizabeth.

Now I cannot presume to speak for a generation, but ultimately I think Taylor's #squad has resonated so much with young women because unlike so much of what they see in the media these days, T. Swift is for her people. On social media, at least (and let's face it—that's a mighty loud voice in the lives of teenagers and twenty-somethings), she seems to support folks wholeheartedly. She celebrates people's accomplishments. She's not afraid to share the spotlight or even step away from it so that someone else can shine.

If "a rising tide lifts all boats," as the famous saying goes, then Taylor is a gravitational force.

She could absolutely compete with the folks who share her sizeable stage every night. She could make up her mind that every one of those women is a threat, and she could feed her own insecurity and selfishness by staking out her territory and erecting "NO TRESPASSING" signs around the perimeter.

However, it seems, at least from my admittedly distant perspective, that she opens her arms, she welcomes, she includes, and she encourages.

So you know what this makes me think, don't you?

Elizabeth and Mary may very well have been our first New Testament #squad, y'all.

Which means that when we look at how they treat one another? When we look at how Elizabeth blesses her younger friend and Mary trusts her older one?

#SquadGoals.

For real.

It's easy to talk about all of this "don't compete / don't compare / everybody be sweet" stuff in theory.

I'll be the first to admit that it gets a whole lot trickier in real life.

Just last night, in fact, I was visiting with a friend at one of my son's football games, and she mentioned that she was fasting from social media. That whole concept is obviously a little foreign to me (hello, blogger), so I asked her why.

"It sounds weird, I know," she answered. "But I get on Instagram and see all the fun things other moms are doing with their kids, and I start comparing like crazy. I feel like I'm not doing enough or not planning enough or not engaging enough with my children. And honestly? It sends me to a little bit of a dark place. I start to feel terrible."

I knew exactly what she meant. Social media might not be my weak spot, but there are about forty-two others. I can hardly read a book, for crying out loud, without thinking of a thousand different reasons why I'm not as good a writer, why I have no business stringing sentences together for a living, why I should never open a new Microsoft Word document for the rest of all time ever.

And there is not world enough and time to discuss how intimidated I can be by people who are consistently achieving #FitnessGoals.

But that is precisely why we need each other, isn't it? It's precisely why it made perfect sense for Mary to go with haste to her older cousin's house—because it serves us well to listen to an actual voice instead of the one that can sometimes scream so loudly inside our heads.

All of this reminds me of a Bob Goff quote I saw one time on Twitter: "We keep pushing people off roofs that we should be lowering them through."[9]

People are hurting, and they're questioning, and they're beating themselves up. They're wondering if God really is calling to something that is miles from their comfort zone. They're doubting if they have what it takes to (fill-in-the-blank), and this current day seems like as good a time as any to ask the Lord to help us speak an encouraging word, to bless the other women in our lives, and to lay down the vast assortment of weaponry that we like to wield against each other in pointless, imaginary battles that no one ever wins.

Beth Moore wrote this (also on Twitter, and you're welcome for all of my super-academic sources, by the way): "This thing we're doing here necessitates a fight. If we drain all our energy fighting people, we'll have nothing left to battle darkness."[10]

Culture tells us to compete. To look out for ourselves.

Scripture tells us to bless. To look out for each other.

The sister in Christ who is standing ahead of us or behind us or even at our own front door is not a threat. She neither hinders nor diminishes the assignment the Lord has given us. But if we let ourselves get sidetracked by pettiness or, heaven forbid, some good, old-fashioned paranoia, we may miss the wonder of seeing how intricately the Lord has woven our stories together, how intentionally He has intersected our paths, and how beautifully our callings complement each other.

Mary and Elizabeth knew a little something about that.

So did Jesus and John the Baptist, for that matter.

It makes me think of Hebrews 10:22–25:

So let's *do* it—full of belief, confident that we're present-able inside and out. Let's keep a firm grip on the promises that keep us going. He always keeps his word. Let's see how inventive we can be in encouraging love and helping out, not avoiding worshiping together as some do but spurring each other on, especially as we see the big Day approaching. (MSG)

As believers and as women, we have no business throwing each other in the Carringtons' lily pond.

Especially when we could be walking the runway together while T. Swift sings "Style."

#SquadGoals, everybody.

Chapter 5

So This Is the Part Where We Need You to Stay in It

My mother-in-law, Martha, is eighty-four years old, and I think it's safe to say that she is remarkable. She never misses church on Sundays or Family Night Supper on Wednesdays. She goes to the beauty parlor every Thursday so that Betty, her stylist for almost thirty years, can wash and set her hair. She meets her friends for lunch on Fridays, and two or three times a week she hops in her sporty four-door sedan and drives to the mall, where she makes the rounds at her favorite stores. She knows her hometown Belk like the back of her hand, and she's not afraid to ask a cashier to call all the other Belks in Mississippi and Alabama to check on something that might not be in stock at her store, whether it's a certain size or a particular color or "that precious New Directions pantsuit! The one in the mail-out! The one with the square buttons that were sort of like pearls, but not *really* pearls, of course, because pearls aren't square, but if pearls *were* square and maybe a little iridescent, they'd look just like these buttons!"

Some people notice eye color or hair styles or speech patterns. Martha notices buttons, and our family is all the better for it.

One of Martha's most endearing traits is her infinite fascination with seemingly insignificant details—like, for instance, the height of a wingback chair or the color of a certain variety of lantana or the texture of a sweater vest in the Boutique section at Stein Mart. In fact, I am fully confident that no matter where I go or what I do, I will never surpass Martha Hudson's endless and utterly sincere interest in, well, practically everything. Take her to Target, and she'll want to know about the varieties of cleaning products they carry and which ones smell the best. Take her to one of her grandchildren's schools, and she'll want to find out where the principal grew up and where in the world she found her perfectly beautiful boots. Take her to a bookstore, and she'll comb the aisles looking for something new by that darlin' author who wrote that darlin' book she read three Christmases ago when we gave her that darlin' poncho, remember?

WASN'T THAT THE MOST DARLIN' CHRISTMAS?

Martha's enthusiasm for life in general absolutely spills into her relationships with her close friends and family, and this is actually the part of her personality that, if you really knew her, would steal your heart forever and always. She's such a faithful caretaker of her people, and I've seen that faithfulness in action as long as I've known her (so, you know, for more than forty years). There have been big, life-altering situations where Martha has cared for others selflessly and sacrificially—both her late husband's battle with cancer and her late mother's decline after a broken hip come to mind—but it's really her day-to-day thoughtfulness that speaks volumes. She checks on folks in the hospital, she sends countless birthday cards, she coordinates meals when there's a need in her Sunday school class.

And on Saturdays, she visits friends who have moved to a nursing home or an assisted living facility.

Yep. She's eighty-four. Visiting friends in the nursing home. EVEN PLAYING BINGO WITH THEM.

Because of course.

Several years ago, in fact, Martha spent the afternoon with a friend who had recently transitioned to a nursing home. Her friend's eyesight and hearing weren't all that great, but Martha didn't let that stop her from jumping right in and doing everything she could for Fran, a woman she'd known for at least sixty years. So Martha read to Fran, and she folded some of Fran's clothes, and she sat with Fran for most of the afternoon. Since Fran couldn't hear very well, Martha had to talk very loudly, and when it was time for Martha to go home, she leaned in closely to her friend and said, "FRAN? SUGAR? FRAN? DARLIN'? I'M GOING HOME! I HAD THE MOST WONDERFUL TIME WITH YOU TODAY! THE BEST TIME! JUST A PERFECTLY MARVELOUS TIME!"

Fran smiled, reached for Martha's hand, and in a flat tone that was just above a whisper, she looked in the direction of Martha's face and confidently said, "Bye, Dot."

Needless to say, Martha was puzzled.

"DOT? I'M NOT DOT! I'M MARTHA! MARTHA HUDSON! THIS IS MARTHA, FRAN!"

"Bye, Dot," Fran repeated.

Martha has always been smart enough to realize when she's fighting an uphill battle. So if Fran was foggy on the finer points of who had been keeping her company, that was just fine with my mother-in-law.

"Bye, bye, sugar," Martha replied. And she left.

But you know what?

She went back to see Fran the very next week.

Martha could have been frustrated, she could have given up, or I guess she could have yelled "MY NAME IS MARTHA" for five or thirty-nine minutes. But she didn't do any of those things. She just kept on keepin' on. She understood Fran's circumstances, she accepted them, and she continued to visit and care for her friend.

She stayed in it.

And that's exactly what I say when people ask me how, at eighty-four years old, Martha manages to do all that she does, how she manages to be so energetic and active and intentional.

She's stayed in it.

At a time in her life when she could sit back and say, "Hey everybody—now it's your turn to wait on me," she chooses instead to serve and love and look out for her people.

And if she could find that suit from the Belk with those square pearl buttons?

Well, then, that would be an extra measure of blessing.

She would look sassier than ever when she visits the nursing homes.

When Elizabeth conceived John the Baptist, she was well beyond child-bearing years, and she was also moving into a stage of life that's probably more associated with winding down than revving up. Granted, life in Judea was much different than it is in twenty-first-century America, but I think there's still a key common thread:

People don't always know how to respond to an older woman who's expecting.

And to be clear, I'm speaking on a couple of different levels here.

Because while yes, a sixty-something woman who's expecting a child in this day and time would probably receive some sort of fast pass into *The Guinness Book of World Records*, there's also the reality that folks are quick to minimize a woman "of a certain age" and assume that her best, most productive, most impactful years are behind her, that she couldn't possibly birth anything new.

And here's the even bigger travesty: women buy into those lies and believe them.

So if I may, let me just hop up on my soapbox, clear my throat, and say something really loudly:

ELIZABETH'S LIFE IS A BEAUTIFUL REMINDER THAT GOD CONTINUES TO DO NEW THINGS IN AND THROUGH US NO MATTER WHAT OUR AGE HAPPENS TO BE.

And don't miss this, either: the calling on Elizabeth's life—in what many would consider her "golden years"—was no small thing (not that there are any small callings, mind you, but Elizabeth's was certainly a visible one when we look back through the lens of history). After all, she was going to be the mother of John the Baptist. She was going to be responsible for raising and teaching the forerunner of Jesus Christ.

And then, when Mary showed up, Elizabeth confirmed her pregnancy. In fact, she confirmed that Mary was "the mother of my Lord," so Elizabeth was the first human in the New Testament to speak not only of Mary's calling—but Jesus', too.

From that perspective, Elizabeth had enormous influence with her young cousin *and* the body of Christ. So when I read Luke 1:41–45 and am reminded again of Elizabeth's strong words of encouragement to Mary, I can't help but wonder, *What if Elizabeth had decided that her Kingdom usefulness was over?*

What if Elizabeth had decided that it was time for her to check out in terms of serving the Lord?

What if she'd gotten fed up with whatever was going on at the temple, crossed her arms, and said, "I'm out"?

What if she had looked at Mary and thought, "Well, I could bless her—but NAH"?

There's just an infinite number of ways we can get burned out and worn down, aren't there?

And let me be clear: if we're truly worn down and worn out, then by all means we need to rest. We're not doing folks any favors when we're trying to serve out of a reserve tank that's already depleted.

But if, for some reason, you have convinced yourself that you're not needed any more, that your best days are behind you, that you're not "relevant" (and that definition seems to change by the day) enough to serve your brothers and sisters in Christ—or, heaven forbid, your family—let me just say this:

Stop it.

Right now.

STOP IT RIGHT NOW.

Don't you dare discount your importance, your influence, or your calling.

And to be clear, I'm oh-so-aware that this kind of doubt can creep up on us at any age. It seems to fire up in my life when I'm in the middle of transition—moving from a comfortable situation to one that requires some bravery, moving from one stage of motherhood to another, moving from one type of service to something new.

But here's what we have to tell ourselves and each other: when we are tempted to give up and hang it up because we're, for whatever reason, fed ALL THE WAY up or maybe just scared to death, we can't forget there are women behind us and ahead of us who need us to stay in it.

There are women in your church who need you to stay in it.

There are women in your family who need you to stay in it.

There are women at your workplace who need you to stay in it.

So you stay in it, do you hear me?

YOU. STAY. IN. IT.

You are uniquely built to impact others in ways you cannot even imagine.

You are the only "you" there is; no one else on earth has your wisdom, your experiences, and your perspective.

So when you're tempted to back down, to back up, or to back off, just remember this:

Elizabeth may have been "of advancing years"—but she was about to birth a whole new thing.

You stay in it.

Right this very second I am sitting in Starbucks.

At the table directly behind me are two precious teenage girls who look to be about sixteen. They're talking 90-to-nothing, interrupting each other in super high-pitched tones, and giggling like crazy.

And while I know that I should be the bigger, more mature person in this situation, it's one of those instances where I'm struggling to be patient. I mean, I came here to find some quiet, to carve out some time to write and think and pontificate (pretty sure that I've never "pontificated" in my whole life, but the word popped in my head, so I ran with it), and for the life of me I can't drown out those two girls' voices—not even when I'm wearing my big ole headphones and listening to The Oh Hellos with the volume cranked up to "stun."

But here's why I need to get over myself ASAP / *tout suite* / PDQ.

Given that the general consensus among researchers is that Millennials were born between 1982 and the early 2000s (2004-ish seems to be as late as most researchers will allow),[11] the girls sitting behind me qualify as members of that particular generation—assuming, of course, that I have guessed their ages with some degree of accuracy. And when it comes to Millennials and the Christian faith—when it comes to Millennials and the church—well, the news isn't too good.

And listen. I'm not much for hand-wringing. I'm not a worse-case-scenario person. I tend to err on the side of optimistic, glass-half-full, get-out-there-and-get-after-a-solution. But if some research I've recently read is a fair representation of Millennials, then the girls sitting behind me in Starbucks?

Well, you'd better believe that I have a vested interest in them. You'd better believe that we all do.

So buckle up, my friends. I'm about to present you with some conclusions that forced me to wrestle with some statistics (that is to say: I was dangerously close to actual math). Suffice it to say that I'm approaching the outermost reaches of my English major comfort zone.

Here's the deal.

A couple of months ago I read a bunch of research by the Barna Group[12] (you can read it too—there's a web address in the notes section), and suffice it to say that church is not the Millennials' favorite place. In general they have some pretty negative connotations about it. They're also wary of Christians and perceive lots of hypocrisy on the part of folks who claim to be believers.

Encouraged yet?

Don't worry. There's a sliver of silver lining.

The Barna Group's research also indicates that Millennials long for community. They long for growth. So in the end, what Barna's data says to me, an admitted failure at any activity that involves decimal points, is that yes, we have a generation of folks in their late teens, twenties, and early thirties who are skeptical, questioning, and maybe even a little bit cynical, but by and large they're not completely closed off to the church. According to Clint Jenkin, Barna's VP of Research, "with all the other options open to Millennials, it's safe to conclude that, when they show up at church for worship or a learning opportunity, they do so hoping that there is Someone present to worship or learn about."[13]

However. Before I wrap up my very short-lived stint in the world of research data, I want to point out two more things that really stood out to me: (1) Young women are increasingly likely to identify as skeptics (atheists or agnostics), and (2) The majority of women who are involved in a church or synagogue state that they feel little, if any, emotional support from their congregations.

Sixty percent feel that way, in fact.[14]

Pardon me while I come in strong with the understatement: THAT IS A LOT.

Certainly I'm no data analyst. Not by the longest shot. But when I look at Barna's research, here's what I know for sure: the gap between women—particularly Millennials—and deep, relational, transformative faith?

It's a big one.

And y'all know the thing about big ole gaps, right? We have to figure out how to build some bridges across them or folks will fall right through the cracks.

Maybe that means you invite a college girl out to dinner.

Maybe that means you send someone an encouraging text or note or card.

Maybe that means you spy a table full of twenty-somethings at a coffee shop—and you pick up the tab.

Bridge building with people outside the church is such a good option, y'all. And it's really not that hard.

By the same token, those of us who are older need to be mindful that Millennial *believers* are the first group of young adult Christ-followers to live in our current post-Christian culture, so they desperately need folks who are a few years/decades/life stages ahead to encourage, teach, disciple, and *listen*.

So for our Millennial brothers, sisters, seekers, and skeptics? We stay in it.

They're walking a tough road. Heaven forbid we let them walk it alone.

Elizabeth, as we know, wasn't too wrapped up in her own life to stop and greet and bless her younger cousin.

And if you ask me, Elizabeth's strongest words to Mary are in verse 45.

Because as I look at verses 41–44 of Luke 1, I'm perfectly content to read them. But when I get to verse 45, I long for a videotape. Or a DVD. Or whatever technology will make me seem less dated and out of it.

I smiled when I typed that.

And regardless of how I wish it had been captured, the reason I want to see it and hear it is because it seems like a moment when someone might put her finger in your face and look you in the eyes and TELL YOU THE TRUTH.

Here's what Elizabeth said in verse 45:

And blessed is she who believed that there would be a fulfillment of what was spoken to her from the Lord.

The Message phrases it like this:

Blessed woman, who believed what God said, believed every word would come true!

And then the Amplified Bible:

And blessed [spiritually fortunate and favored by God] is she who believed and confidently trusted that there would be a fulfillment of the things that were spoken to her [by the angel sent] from the Lord.

Mary Elizabeth Baxter wrote, "[Elizabeth] could not have said to Mary, 'Blessed is she that believed,' except she herself had been 'strong in faith, giving glory to God.'"[15]

Elizabeth could give away wisdom because she had it. And Mary needed it.

Over the last couple of years, I've thought a lot about how God designed those two paths so they would intersect, and *He's done the same thing for us.* The areas where we are wise are meant to intersect with someone else's questions. The areas where someone else is wise are meant to intersect with our questions.

And listen. It may very well be that you identify more with Mary in this particular passage—not in the whole giving-birth-to-a-Savior way, of course, but in terms of knowing that the Lord has laid an assignment on your heart. So if you're not entirely sure what it means or what you're supposed to do—or maybe if you're wondering if you can trust it, if you made it up—this would be a fine time seek out and soak up the counsel of older, wiser women in your life.

I don't know about y'all, but so many times I have flailed and floundered because I resisted guidance. I've shut people out and shut people down before they've ever had an opportunity to speak over or speak into my circumstances.

And I'm done with that, by the way. It's a dumb way to live. Yes, it's vulnerable to open up about the deepest desires of our hearts, not to mention our sins and our shortcomings, but it's better than being isolated. It's better than being bitter.

And it's better than being Zechariah and sitting in silence because we refuse to believe.

Dr. Ralph Wilson writes, "God provided Elizabeth to Mary as a kind of spiritual grandmother . . . who would nurture her and encourage her in the Lord. Elizabeth was her instructor and teacher, her friend and confidant, her mentor and advocate. God gave Elizabeth to Mary for a special period of time and a special purpose. . . . I can't help but think that God may have these roles for each of us, too."[16]

He absolutely does.

And you know the Millennials we were just talking about?

What are we going to model for them and the generations behind them? Are we going to pass on a culture of honor and blessing? A culture where women are valued for the unique gifts they bring to the body of Christ? A culture where women are supportive of each other, encouraging and kind?

I sure hope so.

Looking out for each other isn't always easy. Caring for each other isn't always convenient.

But if we're ever tempted to throw in the towel, so to speak, we need only consider the generations to come.

They need us, you know.

And oh, have mercy—we need them, too.

Stay in it.

Last Tuesday night Martha and I had a long phone conversation while I was waiting to pick up my son from a meeting. It had been a month, probably, since Martha and I talked, and while I would like to say that I am the World's Best Daughter-in-Law and check in with her four times a week, the fact is that between home and work and school and writing and church and football practices and football games and Scout meetings, our family has been chasing its tail for the last couple of months. Right now, in fact, there's an unfolded pile of clean towels in the den, an unfolded pile of clothes in the kitchen, and enough dog hair on the floor (Hazel seems to have developed an itching issue over the last few days) to knit a decent-sized blanket.

I am not my best housekeeping self at this particular juncture.

So last Tuesday night, when I realized that I was about forty-five minutes early to Alex's meeting, I decided it was a perfect time to catch up with Martha. She picked up the phone on the third ring, and we quickly started to talk our way through a long list of topics: how she was feeling (she'd been under the weather), her latest Sunday school lesson, Alex's football season, my niece's college choice, and what my mama was wearing last Sunday at church.

You know, all the important things.

We were about twenty minutes into our conversation when Martha said, "Sophie? I want to ask you something."

I paused for a second out of curiosity for what her question might be; Martha is rarely serious, but her tone indicated some concern.

"Yes, ma'am?" I finally responded.

"Are you taking care of yourself? Looking out for yourself? Are you getting plenty of rest? I mean, I know you're busy and you love your work and doing all that you do—and don't misunderstand me. I'm so glad you get to write and speak and work with those girls at school. I know you love your girls! And David and Alex, too! But are you making sure that you have some downtime? You can't just go, go, go without a break, you know, and I don't want you to run yourself ragged!"

I'm not gonna lie. My mother-in-law hit the bull's-eye. I had felt so run-down the night before, in fact, that I wondered if I was getting the flu. After cramming six speaking engagements—three of which were out-of-state—into a four-week time period, my admittedly self-imposed pace had taken a toll on me. The traveling had been big fun, no doubt about it, but on top of everything else we had going on, it was probably too much. And after I had spent most of Monday feeling teary-eyed and overwhelmed, I suspected before I ever talked to Martha that I was headed for a full-blown bout with weariness.

I assured Martha that I was really and truly going to get some rest soon, and I meant it. But over the next few days, I pushed those very kind words about taking a little break out of my mind, and every time the roller coaster of any given day would start to slow down, I'd opt to keep my seat and ride again.

And again.

And again.

Which brings me to yesterday.

My friend Anne is about fifteen years ahead of me, and for the last six or seven years, she has been a dear friend. About three years ago I realized that she has also become a very trusted mentor. We never made any sort of formal declaration of mentorship, but she opened up her life to me, and I opened up my life to her, and every few months we get together and talk about ALL THE THINGS.

So yesterday afternoon I saw Anne for the first time in several months, and we were about an hour into our catch-up session when she said, very matter-of-factly, "Hey. Let me tell you what I've been praying for you."

I leaned forward.

"I've been praying," she said, "that you will recognize when the Lord gives you opportunities to rest. Because when I look back on when my girls were young, I wish I'd slowed down a little. I don't regret anything—not at all—but I think it would have been good to breathe more, to not push so hard. So that's what I pray for you. That you'll pay attention when the Lord tells you to slow down."

Well.

Then.

How about that?

I mean, there wasn't any audible sound after Anne finished talking, but in the back of my head, I thought, *Did I really just hear the same advice for the second time in a week? Are Anne and Martha tag-teaming me? Is this what it feels like when God puts a holy BOOM on all the ways I rationalize being overcommitted?*

I sat quietly for a few seconds, and then the strangest thing happened.

I felt relieved.

I felt relieved that two women with some wisdom had called my bluff. I felt relieved that two women who really know me had told me to take my foot off of the gas. And I felt relieved that the

Lord, in His kindness, would prompt those two women to confirm what I already knew—even if I didn't want to acknowledge it.

Granted, it wasn't as dramatic a moment as Mary realizing that Gabriel's prophecy was the real deal, but it reminded me that the Lord cares about all the details of our lives—the big stuff, the little stuff, the seemingly insignificant stuff.

And when we stay in it with Him and with each other, just as Martha and Anne have done, He will empower us to meet each other in the areas where we need some loving care the most.

That's why I'm about to shut this computer and take myself a nap.

"Blessed is she who believed there would be a fulfillment of what was spoken to her from the Lord." Right?

Message received.

Loud and clear.

Chapter 6

The Wonder of the Honoring and the Blessing and the Praising

The thing about writing a book is that it kind of makes me a crazy person.

And really, "crazy" might be too broad a term. Maybe "neurotic" is a better word. "Anxious."

"SOMEWHAT HIGH-STRUNG."

It took me a while to admit this about myself, mainly because when I've worked on books I've preferred pretending that I was very normal and relaxed and lo, even breezy. But the reality is the intense periods of writing can render me a fiery hot mess. I love the process so much, but right now, in fact, I'm sitting in my office at home, and I am a sight: still wearing pajamas at three in the afternoon, sporting strong bedhead game (I'd give myself an 8.5 out of 10), and squinting like I'm looking into the sun because I took out my contact lenses and can't see so well.

As always, I am very professional and refined.

I am also a little bit of a basket case.

And I think, for me, that's always going to be part of this whole process.

Last summer, in fact, I finished my last book, and I was as emotional as I've ever been (including when I was fifteen and listening to "Separate Lives" on repeat while waves of estrogen washed over me). Everything made me cry: sunrises, sunsets, insurance commercials, football games, quality time with our dog, the entirety of a NEEDTOBREATHE concert, a kind word from a cashier at the grocery store, you name it. For whatever reason writing that second book made me feel all kinds of vulnerable, and when I finally turned in the final edits, I had the crushing, crippling realization that OH MY WORD PEOPLE MAY ACTUALLY READ IT.

It's funny how that works.

For probably two months, I walked around feeling like my heart was beating outside my body. I was so relieved to be finished but utterly terrified of what was ahead. And how did that fear manifest in my day-to-day life?

Well, I watched the first five seasons of *The Good Wife* in near-record time.

I can tell you in all humility that I sort of outdid myself in terms of shattering personal viewing records.

Well.

Somewhere in the middle of my post-book recovery and my obsessive *Good Wife* viewing, I went to Memphis with Emma Kate, my best friend from college. We had tickets for a conference led by a friend who happens to be one of my very favorite Bible teachers, and I hoped that the weekend would be a reboot for my word-weary brain.

I'll be the first to admit that the reboot got off to a pretty rocky start. I mean, Emma Kate has loved me like a sister since we were nineteen years old, but I think even she would tell you that I was an unpleasant mixture of punchy and defensive the first night we were there. To use one of Emma Kate's favorite phrases, I was "ill as a hornet." And here's the thing: I *knew* I was out of sorts, but pride had me all bogged down in terms of sharing what was really going on. Because if I had been brave (and humble) enough to vocalize my way-deep-down feelings, here's what I would have said:

- I am worried people won't read my new book.
- I am worried people will read my new book.
- I feel icky that I shared lots of feelings.
- I would really like to eat an entire plate of cheese fries dipped in Ranch dressing.
- I feel unqualified to write a book about anything when I still struggle with so much.

You know. Light and carefree concerns.

Saturday morning, though, I woke up awash in conviction and clarity. Emma Kate and I were able to have a long talk before the morning session, and then the combination of that morning's worship and strong teaching straight from Scripture left my heart more tender and pliable than it had been Friday night. That was a very good thing considering that, as my mama would say, I'd been turned wrong side out for longer than I cared to admit.

The event was over right around noon, and before Emma Kate and I met my brother and his family for lunch, I had a few minutes to visit with Beth, my friend who taught. We hadn't seen each other in a while, so as soon as we hugged, she said, "Sophie! Oh my goodness! You finished your book!"

And y'all, as much as I tried to hold it together, I fell apart. In the most embarrassing way, I fell completely apart. I went straight into the ugly cry, and I think I may have even hiccupped.

Clearly my response is evidence of the easy sophistication I bring to social settings.

Beth let me cry for a few seconds while she patted my back and I decorated the shoulder of her jacket with mascara. When I finally started to breathe normally, she said, "Hey—what is it? Aren't you happy with the book?"

"NOOOOOO," I answered—and then I couldn't help but laugh as I wiped my eyes.

I felt like I owed Beth an explanation for the tsunami of tears, so I quickly ran through the list of things I mentioned earlier: the fear, the worry, the frustration, etc., and so on and so forth. I don't think I mentioned anything about the cheese fries because a person can only be so vulnerable in a short amount of time. After I got to the end of my list-o-concerns, Beth, who is a few years older but lifetimes ahead of me in terms of writing experience, empathized with me. She understood. She got it.

It was such a relief to know that she got it.

And then she asked me a question.

"Hey," she said. "Do you believe that the Lord gave you the words inside that book you just finished?"

Her directness caught me so off guard that several seconds passed before I answered.

"I do," I said. Because I did.

"Well, then, I want you to listen to me," she said, and she pointed her finger at my heart while she looked me straight in the eyes.

"You trust Him with it," she said. "YOU TRUST HIM WITH IT."

I didn't even know how to respond.

"I've been there," Beth continued. "I know how it feels. But YOU TRUST HIM WITH IT."

Honestly, I was so moved by her mandate that my first impulse was to salute and say, "Yes, ma'am!"

In the end, though, I uttered a phrase that's easy to say but way harder to put into action.

"I will."

And in the days and weeks and months that followed, I must have repeated Beth's words to myself hundreds of times. Those five tiny syllables comforted and affirmed and blessed in ways I never expected.

They still do, in fact.

"You trust Him with it."

Yes, ma'am.

Believe I will.

By verse 46 of Luke 1, I think it's safe to say that Mary had come a long way. In fact, it's almost funny to look back on Mary's reaction to Gabriel's pronouncement earlier in Luke 1. You probably remember this from chapter one, but essentially Gabriel laid out a whole host of details about Mary becoming the mother of the

Savior of the world, and her reaction indicated some uncertainty about how that whole thing was going to play out:

How will this be since I am a virgin? (v. 34)

Given that initial response from Mary, it's all the sweeter to see the state of her heart and her mind in verse 46. There are only eleven verses that separate Mary's initial reaction from what has come to be known as her "Song of Praise: The Magnificat," so in terms of narrative we certainly don't see a wide range of events. There are three verses where Gabriel offered some explanation and shares the news about Elizabeth. In the next verse, Mary surrendered to the Lord's plan ("Let it be to me according to your word"). Then two verses cover Mary's departure and arrival at her cousin's house.

But the five verses that follow?

They result in a pretty remarkable transformation in our girl Mary.

In verse 45 Elizabeth said, "Blessed is she who believed that there would be a fulfillment of what was spoken to her from the Lord," and in verse 46, Mary's Song of Praise begins. Here are her words:

My soul magnifies the Lord,
>and my spirit rejoices in God my Savior,
>for he has looked on the humble estate of his servant.
>For behold, from now on all generations will call me
>>blessed;
for he who is mighty has done great things for me,
>and holy is his name.
And his mercy is for those who fear him
>from generation to generation.

He has shown strength with his arm;
    he has scattered the proud in the thoughts of their
        hearts;
he has brought down the mighty from their thrones
    and exalted those of humble estate;
he has filled the hungry with good things,
    and the rich he has sent away empty.
He has helped his servant Israel,
    in remembrance of his mercy,
as he spoke to our fathers,
    to Abraham and to his offspring forever.
    (Luke 1:46–55)

That's an articulate teenager, don't you think?

Mary was still in the midst of great uncertainty. She still hadn't told her family that she was pregnant. She was still likely to be misunderstood and even ridiculed back home in Nazareth.

But when we look at those words, we can see that she had indeed come a long way, literally and figuratively. She was at peace. She was joyful. She was grateful.

For he who is mighty has done great things for me, and
holy is his name. (v. 49)

Matthew Henry wrote that "God alone is the object of the praise and the [center] of the joy."[17]

Elizabeth had encouraged and blessed in such a way that Mary's perspective shifted to one of deep reverence for her very good God. Isn't that the best?

Verse 56 of Luke 1 tells us that Mary stayed with Elizabeth for three months, which would have been right about the time that

Elizabeth was ready to give birth to John. I can only imagine the camaraderie, the fellowship, and the community those two women enjoyed as Mary settled into the first part of her pregnancy and Elizabeth prepared for the culmination of hers—both of them chosen by God to birth what mankind could have never conceived.

And I would imagine at some point during those three months, Mary and Elizabeth probably realized how much they needed each other. Three months is plenty of time to cover significant relational ground, to learn what makes each other tick, to figure out what gets on each other's nerves, to discover what fears lurk deep beneath the surface, and to hone in on what makes someone laugh until tears run down her face.

Don't miss this, either: It was three months. Just three months. As far as we know they didn't enter into some lifetime covenantal friendship contract. Their closeness was for a season. I think about that all the time with my high school girls; I typically have nine months with my seniors, then some consistent contact their freshman year of college. But by sophomore year, they've typically made a full transition into college life. AND THEY SHOULD. I know my lane in their lives, and I know when that lane typically merges into something else.

That's part of maturing and growing in faith. We don't have to cling to someone in the hopes they'll stick around, because the Lord holds the threads of that friendship. He'll weave them into something new and beautiful when it's time.

Mary and Elizabeth's three months together left a lasting legacy that reminds us what women can do for each other in this present day. We can help each other see the hand of the Lord in unexpected circumstances. We can walk together in joy and peace because we choose to esteem each other in love and honor. We can minister and bless and encourage within and across our generational lines, and we can give great glory to God in the process.

I believe it right down to my toes.

So, if I'm you, and I'm reading this book, and I'm thinking about the women I encounter every single day of my life—the young mamas I see at church, or maybe the older women I see at a fifty-plus luncheon, or maybe a neighbor I really respect—then I'm starting to wonder about how this whole cross-generational thing plays out in the day-to-day.

Because yes, yay for Mary and Elizabeth and all that, but in terms of the here and now, how do we build trust and invest in other generations? What makes those relationships work?

I have some thoughts.

Raise your hand if you're surprised.

First of all, I want to be super-clear about something, and please know that I say this in all love and without a single bit of condemnation: we need to make sure we're in a healthy spiritual and emotional place before we intentionally start pouring into other people. If we're going to gain gospel ground and build relational capital with the generations behind us or ahead of us, we need to make sure we're not asking folks to follow us onto our personal minefields. So if we're in the middle of a particularly challenging battle with brokenness (and listen—I have been there), that's a perfect time for us to put ourselves under the wisdom, counsel, and covering of loving authority. That can be someone on staff at church, a Bible study leader, a Christian counselor, a mentor, etc.

Certainly we don't have to be perfect—we never will be—but we need to be wise.

So. This is an area where we have to have some oversight, some common sense, and some people in our lives that will tell us the truth. If we know that we are in the middle of a personal mess of our own making, that's probably a good indicator that our immediate focus should be on our own spiritual health (as opposed to, you know, leading a new Bible study). Plus, the other side of our sincere repentance will more than likely be a place where meaningful ministry happens.

Sorry if that was some serious overexplaining, but it's something I didn't understand even a little bit when I was younger.

Now. With the big giant disclaimer behind us, I think probably one more very obvious disclaimer is in order: I do not have all the answers. I don't even have a hundredth of the answers. I just have some experience as a Mary and as an Elizabeth, so we will pretend at this juncture that experience is enough and then pray that the Lord brings whatever clarity we need.

All righty. Here are five things that, in my opinion, will leave a cross-generational friendship dead in the water.

1. **Assumptions and assorted judgments:** Maybe it's *Ohhhhhh—your parents divorced when you were five? I SEE.* Or maybe it's *I see how it's hard to know these things when you didn't grow up in a theologically sound church.* Or maybe—and here's a real humdinger—it's *Well, I'm just thankful that after my kids were born, I didn't have to*

go back to work like you did; I had the luxury of focusing on what really mattered. If we're going to build trust with people, we have to be a safe place (please see: Elizabeth). We're not safe places when we're the ones launching a thousand tiny missiles under the banners of "perspective" and "concern." Tread carefully.

2. **Refusal to meet people where they are:** If we are only ministering to people who have the handy "Sanitized for Your Convenience" strip wrapped around their hearts and minds, then we're probably missing the people we want to serve. We've got to be willing to step into people's messes and love them right there. Jesus was a pretty good model for us, you know?

3. **Generational stereotypes:** Yes, I totally get it if you think, for example, that everyone from Generation X has a bent toward cynicism even though they grew up on a steady diet of Pop Rocks and power ballads. But it's probably better to keep that to yourself until you've earned enough relational capital to voice it without being misunderstood.

4. **Rigid methods:** I am all for being orderly and efficient, but being overly task-oriented as a mentor (or the person being mentored) is a joy-killer. I know it flies in the face of some of our type-A tendencies, but following a checklist very rarely leads to deep, rich relationship.

5. **Unreasonable expectations:** If you're a younger woman, know that being mentored won't fix all the things. And if you're the older woman speaking into the life of a younger woman, know that it's not your responsibility to fix all the things. God may not fix all the things on your watch.

Yes, "All Scripture is breathed out by God and profitable for teaching, for reproof, for correction, and for training in righteousness" (2 Tim. 3:16), but people are not necessarily going to be "equipped for every good work" within a six-month span of time. We need to be diligent, but we also need to be patient with each other.

So there's that.

And while I am not the boss of you, in my experience there have been five things to help make connection easier, especially when we're talking about connecting across generations.

1. **Shared interests:** You like to cook? I like to cook! You like to watch sixteen episodes of *Diners, Drive-ins, and Dives* in a row? SO DO I! Shared interests bridge generation gaps and give us common ground regardless of age. They're not essential for folks to establish a relationship—sometimes opposites attract—but they provide a comfort zone I find really helpful. Shared interests are good.

2. **Genuine friendship:** I'm one of those people who knows almost right away if I'm compatible with someone and if we "click" on a friendship level. The folks who I consider mentors in my life right now were dear, trusted friends before I started turning to them for advice and counsel. Genuine friendship often compels us to meet and talk and listen and learn out of joy instead of obligation. It's key.

3. **Regular, low-pressure contact:** Hear ye, hear ye: It's so important to communicate regularly, but it's not necessary to communicate daily. It's certainly not necessary to *talk* daily; in fact, for many people born after 1980,

the thought of a daily phone conversation will STRESS SOME FOLKS OUT. The important thing is that there's at least a little bit of rhythm to meeting together; when women are at different stages of life, their schedules can be vastly different. Without some type of plan, it's easy for personal contact to fizzle. So yes to being accountable to meet, but no to blowing up someone's phone/e-mail/texts/courier pigeon.

4. **Fun and laughter:** I'm not saying you have to, like, dress up in matching costumes and put on a skit. I'm just saying laughter is the glue that binds hearts together. Well, that and the Holy Spirit. But there's something so liberating about being able to throw your head back and clap your hands with somebody. Yes, we need to bless and encourage and honor. We also need to hold our sides and wheeze a little bit. I'm pretty sure it's biblical. And you'll never convince me that Mary and Elizabeth didn't get *real* tickled every once in a while. I have to think that at some point one of them tripped over her robe and the other one laughed so hard that she wet her pants. This is what women do. This is how we bond.

5. **Extravagant grace:** We are all flawed. We are all broken. We're going to hurt each other's feelings. We're going to say dumb things. We're going to battle a six-day PMS attack and maybe snap at somebody every once in awhile. In spite of all that, we are deeply and completely loved by a Holy God. His grace is lavish, and we get to share it with each other. So in the midst of our misunderstandings, His grace is enough. Always.

That's not a complete list by any stretch of the imagination. Clearly. But those first five examples have tripped me up more often than I care to admit, and those last five examples have proven consistently helpful for me in working with teenage girls and navigating my relationships with older women.

Here's why.

Typically if I talk to, say, a younger woman in some state of discouragement regarding her relationship with a leader/mentor, one of those first five things is in play. Standoffs happen there. Distance happens there. Distrust happens there. And ultimately, a whole lot of disillusionment happens there.

But the last five? They have been faithful helpers in terms of gaining trust, developing lasting friendship, and creating a relational environment where the only agenda is the Lord's.

So.

These are my thoughts.

Do with them what you will.

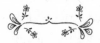

Before we wrap up this section of the book, I want to tell you a little story.

Auburn University's fall break was a couple of weeks ago. And it's totally fine if you had no idea. I don't really expect that many of you have been keeping up with the Auburn academic calendar, but if you have, then KUDOS TO YOU.

Truth be told, I had no idea it was Auburn's fall break until late one Thursday morning when I got a text from one of last year's senior girls. Mamie is a freshman at Auburn now, and her text informed me that she was stopping by my office after she visited with some of her high school friends during lunch.

It probably goes without saying that I was thrilled. After all, it's ever-so-wonderful when kids let you into their lives when they're in high school (I really do count serving high school kids in ministry as one of the greatest privileges of my life), but it's something extra special when those high school kids choose to stay in touch after they go to college.

Seriously. If I think about it long enough I make the "VERKLEMPT" face like Mike Meyers as Linda Richman on *Saturday Night Live* and start waving my hands in front of my eyes to try to stave off the tears.

Sorry to be such an emotional basket case, but apparently this is how I roll.

Sure enough, Mamie popped in my office around 12:15. She was wearing her requisite sorority T-shirt with cutoff shorts and Converse All-Stars, so I grinned that she had the collegiate uniform down pat after only a couple of months. Several other folks from her high school class were with her, and while we were in the middle of a lot of greeting and hugging and "HEYYYYYY"-ing (we're in the South, remember), six or seven more girls walked in. The afternoon was turning into an unplanned mini-reunion, and when several of the guys from their grade walked through my door about five minutes later, I looked at that group of college freshmen, closed my computer, and reminded myself that people trumped whatever happened to be on my to-do list.

For the next two hours they took turns telling me about their classes, professors, classmates, grades, and date parties. I chimed in from time to time, making sure to take a moment to remind them that LEGGINGS ARE STILL NOT PANTS (I am certain that this phrase will be on my tombstone or, at the very least, on the front of the program for my memorial service), but mostly I enjoyed my front-row seat at The Freshmen Show.

It was the biggest blast.

Every time I looked over at Mamie, though, I could tell that we weren't even scratching the surface of what she really wanted to talk about.

By the time everyone started to file out and head off in different directions, it was getting close to the end of the school day. We all exchanged hugs (again), and I had just shut my door and settled into my desk chair when my phone dinged at me.

It was a text from Mamie.

> Can I come back to the school
> tomorrow and talk to you?
> It's fine if you're too busy.
> Just let me know.

I looked at my calendar and realized that the day was pretty full, so I texted her with the only option I had.

> You want to come up here early-ish?
> 8? Too early? I have something at 9:30.

She answered me maybe three minutes later.

> I can be there at 8!

When I read that text, I knew that Miss Mamie meant business. She *really* wanted to talk. Because here is what I know for sure: if a college freshman volunteers to be anywhere at 8 o'clock in the morning, it is typically because (1) someone has promised free food, or (2) there is a significant amount of cash money at stake.

I had offered neither, but Friday morning, when Mamie and her BFF Allison showed up a little after 8:00, they did bring me a Chick-fil-A biscuit.

(You know how people who go to awards shows like the Emmys or the Oscars get Swag Bags? Goody bags full of expensive jewelry and perfume and chocolates and such?)

(Well, that's what a Chick-fil-A bag is to a teacher. It's #TeacherSwag, and it's awesome.)

Mamie and Allison ended up staying for an hour and a half. I wish that I could tell you that our conversation was deeply profound, but it wasn't. It was just real life. We covered topics from choices to identity to flare jeans to Jesus to vulnerability to Instagram. Occasionally they asked for advice, but mostly they just wanted to share all the stuff piled up in their heads and their hearts. So I listened. Sometimes I disagreed with them, but mainly I tried to affirm them. We laughed a whole bunch. And we prayed.

Here's why I tell you all of that.

All too often we fall into thinking that if we're going to have a voice in the lives of younger women, then we need to have all the answers. We need to have earned our certificate as Wiser Older Person. We need to have memorized significant portions of the New Testament, and we need to have a strong theological position on the book of Romans that we're prepared to share in parallel bullet points.

With all due respect, that is a bunch of bull.

Garbage.

Bunk.

Don't get me wrong. I'm all for going deeper in our faith. I'm all for studying the Word and challenging ourselves to know why we believe what we believe. I'm all for being able to instruct and correct and everything else Paul lays out for us in 2 Timothy. Absolutely.

But at the end of the day, we're equipped to minister to each other if we have three things: (1) a way to communicate—like a voice or some handwriting or a keyboard or some ears, (2) the Bible, and (3) the Holy Spirit.

Well, and my mama would want me to remind you not to underestimate the power of a really good cobbler.

I don't know. We can sit around and wait to finally feel "ready" or "qualified" to be that older, wiser voice in a young woman's life, or we can open the Bible and open our hearts and SHOW UP FOR SOMEBODY. This whole process of stepping into each other's lives isn't nearly as complicated as we try to make it. It's relationship. It's friendship. It's fellowship. It's discipleship.

And ultimately, it's not for us. It's not for other people. It's for Him. Forever and only and always for Him.

Mary greeted. Elizabeth honored.

Elizabeth blessed. Mary praised.

They couldn't have known how much they would need each other.

But it sure would have been a shame if they had missed each other.

The same is true for us, too, you know.

Giddy up.

Ruth and Naomi

Chapter 7

When Your Mother-in-Law Is Your Ride or Die

When I was a senior in high school, I signed up to participate in mock trial.

Yes. You read that correctly. *Mock trial.*

To this day I couldn't tell you why I decided to join the pretend-courtroom fun. Because did I want to be a lawyer one day? No. Did I enjoy conflict? Not at all. Did I dream of constructing the perfect cross-examination? Not so much. Did I harbor a secret love and zeal for the law? No, I did not. I mean, sure, I liked to watch *L.A. Law* as much as the next person, but that was really more about seeing Harry Hamlin and Corbin Bernsen and their very fancy late-'80s/early-'90s suits.

Nonetheless, I loved Mrs. Glover, the mock trial sponsor, and I liked to write better than almost anything, so I signed up and told myself that it would be a great learning experience. A week or so later, I met Mrs. G and my mock trial colleagues for our first informational meeting at the county courthouse. A local attorney showed us around and briefed us in regard to our schedule and research.

(Please note my masterful use of legal-ish term "briefed.")

(Clearly I was a mock trial natural.)

About the time the attorney said the word "research," I realized how much preparation and hard work mock trial would require. And approximately eleven seconds after that realization, I started looking for the nearest exit and thinking, *PEACE OUT, mock trial peeps. It's been real real here in the courtroom, but if it's all the same to you, I'm gonna object to this time-consuming extracurricular activity and head on back to the house.*

The second there was a pause in the proceedings (see what I did there?), I made a break for it. I mumbled an excuse to my friends, ran down the courthouse steps, cranked my car, slammed the gearshift into reverse, and punched the accelerator as forcefully as my bronze Nina flats and my nagging conscience would allow.

I was seventeen years old and fleeing from that mock trial informational session like it was on fire. It was weird for me, that overwhelming certainty that NO, I REFUSE TO DO EVEN A LITTLE BIT OF THIS, because for most of my life I'd stuck with everything I'd started. I'd taken piano lessons and dance lessons since I was in first grade. I was a faithful member of my church, my youth group, and even my high school social club (which, in retrospect, might have been a pretty good thing to quit, but we can unpack that another time). If you wanted someone to stick to a plan and keep her commitments, I was your girl.

But then mock trial came on the scene.

And the morning after my Buick and I rode off into the humid Mississippi evening, I went to see Mrs. Glover and made my withdrawal official: I told her that I wasn't going to be able to participate in mock trial after all.

I quit. My underdeveloped sense of commitment and loyalty won the day.

And it was like a switch flipped.

Bailing on mock trial turned out to be one of the most significant events of my high school years, because it is precisely when I discovered how much I liked quitting.

In fact, I decided that I was pretty good at quitting.

There was a lot of quit in me after all!

And while there were probably all sorts of things I could have embraced at that point in my life—academic excellence, fitness, Bible study, devoting fewer waking hours to watching old episodes of *Designing Women* on videotape—I threw my arms around quitting like it was a long-lost friend I'd been missing most of my life. If anything bumped up against my personal comfort zone, I screamed "I QUIT" as I pulled the metaphorical pin and cast that thing out of my routine and my life like a live grenade.

It wasn't a short-lived pattern, either; I was a certified, licensed, and accomplished quitter for the next six or seven years. And while I won't bore you with a detailed list of my quitting accomplishments (which, for the record, might be more widely referred to as, you know, *failures*), I definitely made up for lost quitting time.

(Okay. Here's one example. A couple of years after college I agreed to work with the youth at church, and then, after approximately one Sunday afternoon of sacrificial service,* I never showed up at youth group again.)

(*That was sarcasm. Clearly.)

Over and over I gave myself permission to be flaky and unreliable and selfish (it's not lost on me that you can't spell "quit" without a big, fat "I"). So by the time I was in my early twenties, all that quitting and shortcutting and practicing the fine art of being reliably unreliable—well, it had taken a toll on my mind and my heart. It had affected other people. It had damaged relationships. And it had most definitely interfered in my walk with the Lord.

I wasn't loyal to anyone or anything other than my own dadgum self.

That's why there are still days when I look back over my forty-something shoulder and wish I'd done my late teens and early twenties differently. For sure I get that we're all "prone to wander" people, but wouldn't it be nice if our wandering didn't affect other folks? If we could make our biggest mistakes in isolated, sanitized, vacuum-sealed environments? Wouldn't that be so lovely?

But here's the good news (besides the fact that I dodged having to be a pretend-lawyer, sorry not sorry): in every single bit of that rebellion and shortsightedness, the gentle hand of God stayed right with me, pushing and steering and guiding me toward a better way.

A better Way.

Around 1100 BC, a man named Elimelech quit Israel.

I mean, as far as we know he didn't look at a map of Israel, point, and declare, "I QUIT YOU," but here's what we do know: when his home country was in the middle of a famine, he decided to take a breather from life in the land of Judah, and he moved his family—wife Naomi, sons Mahlon and Chilion—to Moab, a neighboring country on the other side of the Dead Sea.

That means that when things got tough in the Promised Land, Elimelech got the heck out of Dodge—or Bethlehem, as it were. According to David Guzik, Elimelech's departure was "a return towards the wilderness from which God had delivered Israel hundreds of years before. These were clearly steps in the *wrong* direction."[18]

Unfortunately, the wilderness wasn't kind to Elimelech, and he died shortly after settling in Moab. His sons eventually took Moabite wives even though Israeli law forbade them to do so—Mahlon married Ruth, and Chilion married Orpah—and about ten years after their arrival in their new country, both sons died as well.

Given all of that, it seems like Elimelech's decision to move to Moab may not have been his best idea. Yes, life in Israel had been difficult, but the family was intact. After a decade in Moab, though, the family of five was a family of three, and Elimelech's wife, Naomi, was the only original member remaining. But in the middle of her sadness, Naomi—no doubt overwhelmed and unsure of how to move forward—heard that the Lord was once again blessing the people of Israel with abundant crops. It was just the encouragement she needed to set off on a return trip to Judah, her home.

However, the Naomi who was returning to Bethlehem was vastly different than the Naomi who had left over ten years before. Her husband had taken her "from a place where God was honored to a land so heathen in its ways."[19] And after Elimelech's death, any notions that Naomi may have had about being her sons' sole priority were put to rest when Mahlon and Chilion married Moabite women who "were not of her people, nor of her faith in God."[20] Then, after her sons passed away and Naomi found herself longing for the Promised Land, she had no one to accompany her on her journey except for Naomi and Orpah, two daughters-in-law who seemingly had no place in Bethlehem.

She had no idea if anyone would be loyal to her in her time of need.

My mama would say that Naomi was in a real pickle. She had suffered one setback after another, and the circumstances surrounding her return trip to Bethlehem could have been the first Middle Eastern reality show if there had been anything remotely resembling TVs or broadcasting or, I don't know, *electricity* back then.

Two daughters-in-law.
One mother-in-law.
A thirty-mile hike around the Dead Sea.
WHO WILL SURVIVE?

I was in the middle part of my twenties when I realized that it was time to stop being such a flaky fool (side note: all I can think about right now is that "The Flaky Fool" sounds like a bakery for wayward pastries and maybe even rebellious biscuits). And a couple of years after I hit the Real-Live Grown-Up reset button, David and I started dating pretty seriously. Within six months we were engaged, and six months later we were married, and hey, apparently the Lord had helped me make some strides in the way of keeping commitments because MARRIAGE.

Marriage brought all sorts of changes into my life, but I can honestly say that one of the most entertaining parts of being a newlywed was my new mother-in-law, Martha, a silver-haired, five-foot, hundred-pound dynamo who likes to say things in threes and is cute as a button (which is perfect since she also loves buttons).

She does!

She really does!

There are just so many cute buttons!

I consider myself so fortunate to have known Martha Clair Hudson for most of my life. Our families have gone to church together since I was in second grade, so there's no question that I initially took her great affection for my sister-in-law, Rose, and me totally for granted. By the time David and I got married, in fact, Martha had already loved and looked out for me for twenty years, so there was no awkward getting-to-know-you phase in our relationship. I was up to speed on most of the Hudson history before I was officially part of the family, and since David and I had been close friends since we were in junior high, I was as comfortable at Martha's house as I was at my parents'.

As a newlywed, that was such a gift.

My husband and I have now been married for nineteen years, and here's what blows my mind: over the entire course of those nineteen years, Martha has never said an unkind word to me. Not one single time. That doesn't mean that everything has been perfect—family life never is—but even when she has been frustrated or confused or hurt by something I've said or done, she has only responded in the most gracious, loving, and merciful ways. She's quick to tell Rose and me how much she loves us, how proud she is of us, and how she just never dreamed she'd have daughters-in-law she loves as much as us.

In other words, Martha is way more than I deserve.

It's true!

It's really true!

I promise that it's true!

Before they got too far into their trip to Bethlehem, Naomi gave Ruth and Orpah an out. In fact, she told them to "go, return each of you to your mother's house" (Ruth 1:8), and when they refused, she twice pleaded with them to "turn back, my daughters" (vv. 11–12).

(Apparently Martha isn't the only mother-in-law who tends to say things in threes.)

Considering that the women's reaction to Naomi's requests was to cry and "lift up their voices" (vv. 9, 14), it's obvious that they all cared deeply for one another. And the issue at hand wasn't that Naomi didn't want her daughters-in-law to make the journey with her; instead she was essentially saying that they had all been through enough already. After suffering because of Elimelech's choices, she didn't want the young women to face any additional hardships as a result of relocating to Naomi's homeland.

From that perspective, Naomi's deep vulnerability—her admonition to "turn back"—almost seems like she was trying to make right what Elimelech got wrong. Maybe on some level she wanted Ruth and Orpah to do what her family didn't, to do what her family should have done. She wanted her daughters-in-law to stay home while they still could. Because as Naomi knew all too well, once they crossed the border into a foreign land, it could be a very long time before they got to go home again.

In Ruth 1:8–13, there's an incredibly emotional exchange between the three women. Naomi gave them every opportunity to walk away, and in Ruth 1:14, we see what Naomi's daughters-in-law finally decided to do.

"And Orpah kissed her mother-in-law, but Ruth clung to her."

In what must have been an absolutely agonizing decision, Orpah's kiss signaled her departure from the trio and her intention to stay in Moab. Maybe that's why those last five words of verse 14 carry so much weight and pack such relational punch; Orpah was leaving, "**but Ruth clung to her**" (emphasis mine).

Naomi made one last attempt to get Ruth to change her mind, but Ruth was resolute:

> Don't force me to leave you; don't make me go home. Where you go, I go; and where you live, I'll live. Your people are my people, your God is my god; where you die, I'll die, and that's where I'll be buried, so help me GOD—not even death itself is going to come between us! (vv. 16–17 MSG)

It's one of those passages that takes my breath away a little bit, because it's a level of commitment we don't see modeled often in our current culture. Ruth wasn't trying to appease Naomi with her words, and she wasn't giving lip service to make herself look good; she was pledging the rest of her life to her mother-in-law and letting her know that Ruth + Naomi = LONG HAUL. The age gap didn't matter, the family devastation didn't matter, the difference in backgrounds didn't matter. There was nothing "fair weather" about this relationship, nothing conditional about her loyalty.

Verses 16–17 really are such a beautiful reminder of what sacrificial, committed care for our people looks like. As Matthew Henry wrote, "Nothing could be said more fine, more brave, than [Ruth's words]. She seems to have had another spirit, and another speech, now that her sister had gone, and it is an instance of the grace of God inclining the soul to the resolute choice of the better part."[21]

Then there's this:

WHEN we STICK TOGETHER in TOUGH TIMES—WHEN we CHOOSE TO WALK THE ROUGH ROAD TOGETHER instead OF LETTING circumstances SPLINTER us APART—We can't even imagine HOW THE LORD MIGHT redeem THE PARTS OF OUR RESPECTIVE STORIES THAT ARE difficult and MAYbe even PAINFUL.

But that's precisely what Ruth and Naomi were about to find out.

About seven years ago Martha and I took a little road trip of our own to a ministry event in Memphis. While I was going to do some blogging work, I knew the weekend would also be loads of fun, and I had originally planned to drive over by myself. A couple of weeks before the conference, though, I felt super convicted that I was supposed to ask Martha to go with me. Never one to turn down an out-of-town adventure (unless it interferes with her standing appointment at the beauty parlor), Martha was immediately on board, and late one Thursday afternoon, we set out on the four-hour trek from Birmingham to Memphis.

On the surface, everything was peachy and rosy and whatever other color has a happy connotation, but there was a whole lot bubbling under the surface that Martha didn't know about. David was feeling all sorts of pressure related to his work; we were both trying to navigate our respective stages of marriage and parenting; and between juggling a return to full-time teaching as well as some freelance writing, I spent most days feeling overwhelmed and maybe a smidge resentful that I had so much on my plate. There was a near-constant pit in the center of my stomach and the most annoying nag in the back of my brain. It was almost like a mixture of fear and dread formed a tiny mental cloud that stayed with me all the time, and nothing I did seemed to make it budge.

I couldn't make that sucker rain, either. Not for love nor (lack of) money.

So there I was, driving my mother-in-law up Highway 78, feeling sick at my stomach whenever I thought about the Assorted Problems and Also Pressures of 2009. Martha, on the other hand, was in fine form, and it didn't take long for me to realize that there were three specific topics she wanted to discuss: (1) the floor plan of her new patio home, (2) her search for a new sofa, and (3) the elusive nature of a three-piece patio set.

So I think it's safe to say that Martha and I weren't exactly in the same frame of mind.

For the first couple of hours, I played the sweet daughter-in-law game really well. And don't misunderstand: I *wanted* to be the sweet daughter-in-law. Martha is a gem, and I really did (and do) want to honor her and love her well. So I paid attention as she walked me through the details of the floor plan, I looked at the envelope where she'd drawn out potential furniture placement in her living room, and I nodded as she talked about the perils of oversized furniture ("Sofa cushions are so big now! They're just so big! I mean, Sophie, CAN YOU EVEN BELIEVE how big sofa cushions are?!"). We lamented the difficulty of finding a small-ish wrought iron patio set to fit on her back porch, and then we segued into a lengthy conversation about antique tea carts and how perfect it would be if Martha had one in front of her kitchen window.

Martha wanted to put a lamp on it!

Just a cute little lamp!

It would be so fun if the tea cart had a lamp!

As we got closer to Memphis, though, I could feel that nag of fear and dread threatening to take over, which meant that Martha's lighthearted conversation and furniture plans and patio set dreams started to feel like a really cute shoe that I'd been wearing for about an hour too long. It was pinch-y and rubbing me the wrong way; plus, I wanted to talk about real problems and maybe not quite so many things involving the Sunday circulars from furniture stores.

See? I am a terrible, petty person.

(Also, if you read the previous chapter, let me ask you this: what is it about Memphis being my go-to location for emotional come-aparts while attending Christian conferences?)

(Perhaps we need to explore this pattern at another time.)

(Or maybe I just need to quit going to conferences in Memphis.)

(Anyhoo.)

I do want to be crystal clear about something: the problem that weekend wasn't Martha at all. The problem was my preoccupation with my own internal turmoil combined with a misguided assumption that my mother-in-law couldn't relate to how I was feeling. To my way of thinking, at least, I was dealing with some Serious Life Pressures, and, as far as I could tell, the biggest issue in Martha's life was where to find an elusive antique tea cart and some smaller-scale sofas.

Martyr much? Because I think I majored in it that weekend in Memphis.

For the next forty-eight hours, I continued to fight the same mental and emotional battle. Oh, I smiled and I played nice and I sang real loud during worship and I underlined passages in my Bible and I took copious notes during the teaching. But my heart was unsettled—irritated, even—and I didn't know what to do with it.

Fortunately, though—mercifully—Martha totally stepped up and bridged the gap. I don't know if she picked up on what was going on with me, but not too far into our Sunday morning drive back to Birmingham, she made a simple, straightforward statement that pierced right through that bubble-o-frustration I'd allowed to settle around my heart:

"Sophie, I've never experienced worship like that in my life, but I needed it, and I sure do thank the Lord for it."

And then: "I just never dreamed I'd enjoy life so much at this age. It's not perfect, and sometimes things are sad, but I'm so blessed. It's more than I ever hoped."

There was a tender vulnerability in Martha's words, and as I looked over at her in the passenger seat, a wave of compassion swept over me. For the first time all weekend, I thought about the reality of her daily life—how she cared for her ailing mother, how she missed her late husband, how she ministered to friends with failing health. I thought about hardships she'd endured, tough situations she'd grieved, and how, in her late seventies, she loved the Lord more than ever.

She had been delightful company on our trip, no doubt about it, but what I didn't stop to realize was she needed a break from the pressures of home just as much as I did. Her unexpected moment of reflection snapped me out of my selfishness and made me remember that she was dealing with so much more than floor plans and patio sets and tea carts. In fact, she was actually managing "a lots," as she's fond of saying, and she was every bit as desperate for Jesus to intercede in her circumstances as I was.

Martha understood way more than I gave her credit for.

About that time she piped up from the passenger seat.

"Sophie, can I ask you something?"

"Sure thing," I said.

"You know your friend Travis? The one who was the choir director or the music minister or whatever you call it at the conference? The one who sings so beautifully?"

"Yes, ma'am," I grinned.

"Do you think you could get me some of his cassette tapes?"

"Well," I laughed, "I could if it were 1992, but since it's 2009, I may have to get you some CDs. Would that be okay?"

"That would be wonderful! Just wonderful! Perfectly wonderful!"

That Martha Hudson—I'll tell you what. She's not big as a minute, she's a devoted fan of the 3/4-sleeve jacket, and she's one of the strongest people I know.

So all of this stuff—the Naomi stuff, the Ruth stuff, the Martha stuff, the hey-sometimes-I-overreact stuff—it has me thinking.

And it reminds me that whether we're older or younger or somewhere in between, we can so easily fall into the trap of looking at other women and thinking, *Well, you are just in a completely different stage of life than I am, and you know what? That annoys me. I may even resent you for it.*

In fact, now that I can look back on that weekend with Martha, it seems clear that my arms-crossed, head-turned, can't-pinpoint-the-disconnect attitude is exactly where the enemy would like to hold us in our relationships with women (maybe even especially older women) who hold a special place in our lives. After all, if we tell ourselves that a person will never understand where we're coming from and what we're dealing with, then odds are we won't open up.

And if we don't open up, we can rest assured that we'll miss out on other women's wisdom and perspective. We might even walk around with a bunch of burdens we shouldn't be trying to carry alone. We might compare ourselves straight into isolation and loneliness.

Or, heaven forbid, we might just quit—quit trying to reach out, quit trying to connect, quit trying to be vulnerable, quit trying to support, and quit trying to love each other really well.

If we're not careful, we'll pour bitterness and condemnation on wounds we should slather with forgiveness and grace.

I can't help but think that we need Ruth and Naomi to school us in some areas where we need to learn a few lessons.

Because when Naomi was as vulnerable as she could possibly be with her daughters-in-law, Ruth didn't think all that baggage was too much to carry. She wasn't deterred by the reality of life with a mother-in-law who had a history of heartache and no concrete plan for the future.

By the same token, Naomi wasn't deterred by the reality of life with a Moabite who had married her Jewish son, a woman who would no doubt face scorn and maybe even shame in Judah simply because of her background.

Facing less than ideal circumstances, Naomi and Ruth were two very imperfect women—one older, one younger, both widowed, both displaced—but they linked arms and joined hearts and committed to walk that thing out together.

There's wasn't a bit of quit in them.

When Ruth and Naomi finally reached the Promised Land, their problems didn't magically disappear. Like it or not, their loyalty and commitment to each other didn't result in surprise sightings of unicorns and rainbows in the immediate vicinity of the Dead Sea.

And when Martha and I finally reached the Birmingham city limits after our weekend in Memphis, we were still dealing with the same individual challenges and concerns we'd taken with us to Tennessee. Unfortunately, Martha couldn't fix what was bothering me, and I couldn't fix what was bothering her. I certainly couldn't make the perfect antique tea cart appear, though if I could have, BELIEVE YOU ME it would have been at the top of my to-do list.

But regardless of the source of our respective problems and fears and worries, and regardless of how those things eventually played out, I knew beyond a shadow of a doubt that while yes, Martha was my mother-in-law, she was also my faithful friend.

And while I might eventually give up on determining the perfect furniture arrangement for her living room, I'd never give up on her.

I mean, how could I?

She's so fun!

She's just too fun!

Of all the mothers-in-law in the whole wide world, she really is the very most fun!

Chapter 8

Never Underestimate the Power of a Good Cleaning

I was in high school when I noticed that a lady named Martha Stewart seemed to be popping up everywhere. Mama had one of her cookbooks, and she was a frequent guest on the morning shows I'd occasionally watch when I was getting ready for school. She also had a Christmas special on PBS, and I remember being utterly fascinated by her crisp East Coast accent along with her affinity for fresh cranberries.

I need to talk about those cranberries for just a second.

As a child of the Deep South, the existence of fresh cranberries was a wonder to me. Back in the '80s it was unusual to see fresh cranberries in Mississippi grocery stores—we mostly bought Ocean Spray in a can—so watching Martha Stewart string cranberries and roll cranberries in sugar and grind cranberries for a vanilla ice cream topping was like stumbling across the customs of a strange and foreign land. Sometimes I couldn't help but think of a line from the old "Unfrozen Caveman Lawyer" sketches on *SNL*: "Your world frightens and confuses me."

There was one year, in fact, when Martha Stewart gave detailed instructions about how to spiral approximately four thousand cranberries (rough estimate, give or take) onto a Styrofoam wreath. Even at my young age I knew that was not going to be at the top of my list for whiling away a winter afternoon, especially after Martha Stewart said that the first step was to gather an obscene amount of toothpicks, break each one in half, and then one by one pierce the cranberries with a half toothpick.

Just thinking about it makes me feel faint.

And now that I'm in my forties, that cranberry wreath project is some version of my worst nightmare. Because do you know how much I could accomplish in the fourteen mind-numbing hours I'd spend breaking toothpicks and piercing cranberries and spiraling them around a Styrofoam wreath? I could fly halfway across the world, for heaven's sake. Or I could watch over half of a season of *Parenthood*. Or I could drive to Target, buy a wreath, drive home, hang it up, and then have thirteen hours left over to do all sorts of glorious things like sleeping or frying chicken or pinning Pinterest recipes that I have no intention of actually cooking.

Also, do you know how long those cranberry wreaths supposedly lasted, according to Martha Stewart? A WEEK.

If I'm going to invest that much time into something, I'm pretty much going to need it to last until Jesus returns, give or take a couple of weeks.

Okay. I'm all done talking about the cranberries now. Clearly I have some feelings.

For the most part I could watch Martha Stewart share recipes and projects and elaborate instructions for wrapping a turkey in puff pastry and keep it all in perspective. As fascinated as I was by her creativity and attention to detail, I certainly didn't harbor any deep desire to follow in her footsteps as a lifestyle expert (which, for the record, was a whole new thing in the late '80s and something none of us knew we needed). Plus, I grew up surrounded by women who entertained effortlessly and beautifully, and I was much more drawn to their old-school vestiges of Southern hospitality than I was to Martha Stewart's tutorials about the wonders of radicchio.

I mean, give me some iceberg lettuce slathered in Comeback Sauce any day of the week, you know?

After I got married, though, Martha Stewart's tips and tricks and ideas resonated with me a whole lot more than when I was a teenager. Suddenly I found myself with my very own china, not to mention an assortment of crystal and flatware that would have made Emily Post proud, and I realized how much I liked setting a pretty table. Combine the staging and accessorizing with my love for cooking (which, by the way, I still love a whole lot), and I unknowingly started to buy into the crazy idea that when David and I invited people over, I didn't just need to welcome them—I needed to entertain in such a way that, at the end of the evening, someone might be tempted to award me a gold medal in the Lifestyle Expert Competition.

The fact that said contest was completely imaginary didn't slow me down even a little bit.

I was in it to win it, y'all.

Typically my pre-dinner preparations started several days in advance with some extensive dog-earing of the latest issues of *Southern Living* and *Martha Stewart Living*. I'm not even sure that I used very many of the ideas that I saw on those pages, but they

for sure ramped up my inner expectations for how perfect everything needed to be. I spent lunchtime at work making the most
detailed to-do lists you ever did see—things like "cut camellias
for mint julep cups," "plant new annuals in front flower bed," and
"make seasonal wreath for front door."

No cranberries, though. I hadn't *actually* lost my mind.

And it's not that any of those things were bad, you understand. My heart just got so fixated on the externals—how pretty
everything should look, how delicious my food should be, how
clever it might be to make bud vases out of acorns—that I totally
missed the internals. I wasn't relaxed, I wasn't ready to listen, and
I certainly wasn't ready to laugh because UPTIGHT MUCH,
FRANCES?

Honestly, I wasn't focused at all on our guests; I was con-
sumed by everything I needed to do *for the dinner.* And oftentimes
when people arrived at our house, I was totally preoccupied with
Other, Very Important Matters because I was probably tweaking
the magnolia branches running down the center of the table or
re-folding napkins or FILLING OUT PLACE CARDS, FOR
HEAVEN'S SAKE.

Because when you have four people over for dinner, it's very
important that you assign seats, my friends.

The fact that I was young and still figuring out what it meant
to take care of our friends and family was probably part of the reason I fell into this pattern. There's definitely a learning curve for
practicing hospitality and caring for others, and on the front end,
it's easy to mix up our priorities.

And the bigger piece of the puzzle, at least for me, was that I
way undervalued the impact of a simple, loving gesture. On some

level I believed I had to set the most gorgeous table in the most beautifully decorated (and cleanest!) house in order for the actual meal (which, naturally, needed to be off-the-charts memorable) to count.

I watched my mama entertain all of my life, but somehow I'd missed what she'd known all along: genuine hospitality doesn't have to be fancy, and it provides for folks in ways that go far deeper than giving them something to eat and drink. Because if I had to guess, I'd say lots of people walked away from my table feeling empty even if their stomachs were full. Sure, I never attempted one of those fresh cranberry wreaths like Martha Stewart made, but in retrospect I'm afraid that I busied myself with equally futile pursuits.

Even still, those magnolia branches were stunning as a centerpiece.

The camellias in the mint julep cups offset them beautifully.

(KIDDING.)

(Only I'm totally serious.)

The last time we saw Ruth and Naomi, they had just arrived back in Bethlehem. Naomi was trying to change her name to Mara since she said the Lord had dealt bitterly with her, and Ruth may or may not have been standing by her mother-in-law's side and contemplating whether it would be rude to tell Naomi to take a chill pill.

To be clear, Scripture makes no mention of Ruth asking her mother-in-law to SIMMER DOWN for a second. All I'm saying is that Naomi was a little bit of a Debbie Downer—maybe just a hair shy of pulling out her Sad Trombone and playing a few notes—which was fair enough, I guess, considering everything she had endured.

But by the beginning of Ruth 2, our friends Naomi and Ruth were more settled. Ruth needed a job (or, as my sister would say, she needed a J.O.B.), and since it was barley harvest time, her plan was to see if she could glean after the reapers. That meant she wouldn't be one of the main workers, but after the reapers gathered the majority of the crop (with the exception of the corners, which Levitical law forbade reapers to cut), the gleaners could go behind them and pick up whatever was dropped or left over. Those uncut corners, "one of the social assistance programs in Israel,"[22] were theirs for the taking, as well.

As it turned out, Naomi's late husband, Elimelech, happened to have a relative, Boaz, who was a landowner, and on her first day as a gleaner, Naomi happened to find her way to his land. Boaz happened to see her and asked one of his workers who she was. That worker happened to know about Ruth's connection to Naomi, and he also happened to be able to testify to the fact that Ruth had worked her tail off that day.

In fairness, there's no translation of the Bible that refers to someone working his or her tail off. But you get the idea.

And yes, that's a whole lot of happenstance at the beginning of Ruth 2. If we didn't know about, you know, the providential hand of God, we might be tempted to think Ruth benefitted from a series of coincidences, but the truth (and the Truth) of the matter is that the Lord was guiding her exactly where He wanted her, working out the details of Ruth's life for her good and His glory.

There were all sorts of encouraging developments after Boaz learned Ruth's identity, chief among which was his willingness to look at her vulnerability as a widow and a foreigner in his fields and essentially say, "Hey. I got this." (Granted, Boaz didn't share a vernacular with, for instance, Ryan Gosling, but his actions very much lined up with an "I got this" attitude.) He told Ruth to stick by the young women who worked for him, he assured her the young men wouldn't bother her, and he invited her to drink freely from the water his young men provided. And then, after he blessed her for her faithfulness to her mother-in-law and asked the Lord to give her a full reward (v. 12), he offered her bread and wine when she sat down for lunchtime.

Boaz's kindness didn't stop there. He instructed his men to let Ruth glean among the sheaves, which meant she could take from the bundles of barley that had already been gathered. He also told them to "accidentally" drop some of what they were harvesting, knowing that she would pick it up as she gleaned behind them. And even though the events of the book of Ruth took place over a thousand years before a man named Paul wrote to the church at Ephesus, the spirit of Boaz's actions and his generosity toward Ruth remind me of Paul's words in the last part of Ephesians 3:20: "above and beyond all that we ask or think" (HCSB).

What strikes me the most, though, is how Ruth was able to bless and care for Naomi as a result of her gleaning. Our current culture would tell us that we have to go big or go home, that we have to be the chief and not the Indian, that we have to be the starter and not the backup. Whether we mean to or not, we sometimes send the message that we value flash over substance, that we prefer the spotlight over behind-the-scenes, that we crave fame over faithfulness.

Just look at our girl Ruth, though. She wasn't on the front lines. She was a gleaner, not a reaper. She worked from morning until night at a job that was far from glamorous, and she did so without any expectation of advancement or preference or reward. As my aunt Chox would say, Ruth just got out there and got after it.

And when she went home after her first day's work, she presented Naomi with far more than she could have imagined: an ephah of barley (almost five gallons)[23] plus the leftovers from her lunch with Boaz.

To some people it might not have seemed like much at all, but it was an abundance of riches for a widowed foreigner and her mother-in-law.

And the harvest wasn't over yet.

If I had to guess, I'd say a lot of us are putting some serious pressure on ourselves to be all things to all people.

WHOOOOOOOA, Nellie, you're probably thinking. *I must have forgotten the part where I asked you to get all up in my business.*

But I know what my life looks like. I know what my friends' lives look like. And I think it's safe to say that maybe—just maybe—we all need a nap. And perhaps a restorative massage.

Just last week, in fact, a friend of mine—I'll call her Katherine—gave me the rundown of what she and her family had going on over a week-long span, and by the time she got to the end of the list, I felt like a cartoon character whose eyeballs had started to spin. Katherine works part-time, so in addition to the necessity of shuttling two kids to the week's school and sports practices and dance lessons and doctor's appointments and church activities, she also had a couple of after-hours job-related events that were nonnegotiable.

On top of that, she and her husband, who travels frequently for his job, were making a late-week out-of-state trip to celebrate an extended family member's graduation, but they had to drive home early the following afternoon for their older child's basketball doubleheader. On Sunday they wanted to carve out a tiny pocket of family fun somewhere in between going to church, singing in the choir, and attending small group—but Katherine said that most Sundays, when they finally stagger through the back door, they have just enough time to eat supper, wrap up any loose ends with the kids' homework, coordinate schedules for the next week, and prepare to start the process all over again.

I told Katherine that her life makes me tired.

She said that was fine because my life makes her tired, too.

And if we're honest, we'd have to say that many women feel like they're drowning (or maybe juggling knives is a better description). It could be that they're mamas taking care of their obligations in the midst of changing diapers or playing Chutes and Ladders for the 452nd time (be near, Lord) or coordinating the local elementary school's Fall Festival despite the fact that they have spent the last eight years begging and pleading for a reprieve from the PTA leadership team, PLEASE, JESUS, MAKE IT SO.

And don't even get me started about how much my homeschooling friends have on their proverbial plates. Suffice it to say that it's enough to make lesser women (like myself, for example) pick up that overcrowded plate and sling its contents off the front porch before introducing said plate to the transformative power of a hammer.

(Come to think of it, maybe we all just need to pause right now and enter into a brief season of prayer on behalf of our home-schooling friends.)

(Because NO BREAKS, PEOPLE. NO BREAKS FROM THE PRECIOUS ANGEL CHILDREN.)

And listen. It's the same deal if you're single, if you're kid-free, if you're empty nesting, if you're a Millennial, or if you're a Baby Boomer.

Life is full.

So given all of that, there's no doubt time is always precious—no matter what your season of life happens to be. But sometimes time seems flat-out scarce when you're facing a seemingly endless rotation of responsibilities.

And for most women, whether we like it or not, there's just not a whole lot of margin in the day-to-day.

So I think all of this fairly begs the question: Considering how full the day-to-day can be, where do we find extra hours so we can look out for each other? Take care of each other? Minister to each other?

I mean, if our families and our jobs and our etceteras demand so much of our time and energy, does that mean we're supposed to put on blinders and ignore needs with our extended families and friends? Turn a blind eye to whatever is going on in our communities?

You know the answer as well as I do: *of course not.* I mean, every once in a while we may need to close ranks and circle the wagons when our families are working through something deeply personal or trying to heal from something deeply painful.

But more often than not—if we're in healthy community and relationship—we're going to walk through life with all sorts of folks. And I think we can take a hint from Ruth when we're trying to find extra measures of both margin and provision.

So if you're wondering, *WHERE? WHERE DO I FIND THEM?*

Well, the "where" is pretty simple.

Where else? In the gleaning.

When I was younger, I watched Mama and my aunt Chox take incredible care of their parents. They took them to their doctor's appointments, stayed with them in the hospital, and helped them however they could. Chox worked full-time at their family business and Mama stayed at home (where she excelled at keeping the most gorgeous home you ever did see), so they tag-teamed to fit their schedules and did whatever Mamaw and Papaw needed them to do.

From my perspective, Mama and Chox handled their parents' care in the most casual, effortless way. They just made a few phone calls, drove to the hospital every once in a while, and talked to doctors whenever it was necessary. Super simple. Not much to it.

Well.

Let's just talk about that whole "casual, effortless" thing, shall we?

I mean, my goodness. The last few years have taught me some lessons about that. Cleared up some misconceptions, you might say. I think Sister and my cousin Paige would agree. Because as our mamas have gotten older, as they've faced various health challenges and endured more than we ever imagined they'd face, we've learned what a big job Mama and Chox had as they cared for Mamaw and Papaw.

That job is an honor.

But that job can also take a toll.

Paige was the first one of the three of us to walk that road. About ten years ago her daddy, our Uncle Joe, was diagnosed with Alzheimer's, and then a couple of years before he passed away, doctors diagnosed Chox with cancer. She's done remarkably well considering that she's been fighting to get better for six years, and if you asked her how she's doing, she'd say, "Oh, I'm fine—just fine. There are other folks who have it way worse. Now what do you know good? Tell me something funny."

More than anything else on earth, Chox loves to laugh. I appreciate that in a person.

If you pressed her, though, and asked her the worst part of her illness, she say, "those treatments"—and then she'd roll her eyes. She takes injections every few weeks, and while the injections have done a good job of stabilizing the cancer, they sometimes cause side effects. As my brother-in-law Barry would say, those side effects are a whole 'nother kettle of fish. Paige has pretty much whittled the timing of them down to a science, so whenever they hit hard, Paige takes her mama to the emergency room, sits with her through the night, stays until Chox gets moved to a room, and then runs to work for as many hours as she can before she goes back to the hospital to spend the night.

This is precisely why I ask Paige one question more than any other: "Are you getting any sleep?"

Paige never answers. She just laughs.

I don't know exactly how many times Chox and Paige have repeated their side effects song and dance over the last six years, but let me put it this way: the side effects song and dance is, at the very least, old enough to vote. Around the fourth or fifth time it happened, I asked Paige if the hospital might let her have a garage door opener that she could push once she got in range of the emergency room—something that would automatically open doors, call for an orderly, and admit her mama. At the time we laughed at that idea, but since then they've been back so many times that the button just makes good sense. It's a matter of efficiency.

So the hospital and Chox? They're pretty familiar with each other.

Which means Paige and vinyl fold-out sofas are pretty familiar with each other, too.

As you can imagine, Chox and Paige would probably tell you that repeated hospital stays = Happy Fun Times but only if it's Opposite Day. So it might seem weird when I tell you that when I think back on Paige's stories about her trips to the hospital with Chox, I'm reminded of the power of gleaning.

(Seriously.)

(I'll stop for just a second so that you can rub your neck in an attempt to alleviate the symptoms of the topical whiplash I just caused.)

(I have some Icy Hot in my purse if you need to borrow it.)

All righty.

Here's the thing about the gleaning: we totally underestimate its value when we're in the middle of something difficult. However, I am here to declare forever and for always that when tough times hit—and they will—GLEANING IS THE BOMB. Ruth could attest to that, couldn't she? I mean, she and Naomi were in a tough spot, and Ruth had to work in the fields as a means of survival, and out of the leftovers of the harvest, all of Ruth and Naomi's needs were richly supplied. Ruth faithfully gleaned, and they ended up with more than they needed.

In the case of Chox's multiple hospital stays, gleaning has been oh-so-significant even though the gleaning had nothing to do with, say, *barley*. Instead gleaning has meant that friends and extended family members found leftover time in their very busy schedules to stop by, to text, or to call and say *Hey, we see you. Hey, we love you. Hey, we're praying for you.*

Or even *Hey, Paige, we're going to bring you an Icee because we know that hospital has the heat cranked up to a temperature that rivals the surface of the sun, and an Icee will do wonders when you feel like you're crawling through a thick cloud of hot.*

Nobody has ever arrived at Chox's hospital room door with a manual entitled *Now I Will Solve All Your Problems.* Nobody has camped out with Paige on the sofa bed in a dramatic show of solidarity (and even if they tried, Paige wouldn't let them because those bed springs leave indentations on your liver, for heaven's sake).

But Chox's and Paige's friends and family members glean like crazy. During what could be regarded as "throwaway" time—five minutes here, twenty minutes there—they glean on their behalf.

They gather and harvest seemingly insignificant moments during those hospital visits to love and care for Chox. They drop off flowers, they make sure Chox has plenty of crushed ice in her water mug, they text to let Paige know they're praying, they leave voice mails offering everything from food to pajamas (in the event that Chox and Paige are ill-prepared for a few nights of Hospital Camp). They keep Chox company, laugh with her, and sit by her bed so Paige can meet her husband for dinner or go to her son's T-ball game. People glean the minutes that could easily be squandered or ignored.

And Paige would say that she will never forget how lavishly and generously the Lord has provided through their faithfulness.

Anyone who has spent time in a hospital knows that when you're finally dismissed, you're forever grateful for the front-line reapers—the doctors, the nurses, the lab techs—who dedicate considerable energy and resources to helping you or someone you love get better.

But from a purely relational perspective, do you know what will continue to inspire and encourage and comfort us when we look back on tough times?

The profound power and provision of the gleaning.

Ruth was on to something, y'all.

Chox and Paige will attest to that.

There are more than three thousand years between Ruth's life in Bethlehem and our current twenty-first-century existence, and

I'll be the first to admit that sometimes it's way easier to focus on our differences instead of our similarities.

For instance, Ruth couldn't open a laptop and Google "stuck in foreign land with cranky mother-in-law" and find instant empathy on no fewer than forty-five message boards devoted to that specific topic. Ruth couldn't throw on some shoes and walk to the closest Starbucks if she was craving a little "me time."

Come to think of it, Ruth was probably wholly unfamiliar with the concept of "me time."

Ruth couldn't put on her headphones and crank up her iTunes if she wanted to block out the noise of the world. She couldn't run by Kroger if she was iffy about what to fix for dinner. She couldn't open her Netflix app and mindlessly watch every single episode of *Friends* or *Gilmore Girls* or *The Office*.

Given my lifelong affinity for television and all of its treasures, it is difficult for me to imagine a civilization where this was the reality. It is neither just nor fair. The mere fact that Ruth and her girlfriends never knew the joys of quoting Joey Tribbiani sort of makes me want to get back in the bed.

(Actually, it makes me want to say, "Hey Ruth—how YOU doin'?")

For Ruth, there was no distraction from the immediacy of her needs. There was no escaping the realities of the very real pressures she and Naomi were facing. But as she gleaned, the Lord made a way. He didn't just take care of the essential physical needs, either. Sure, Ruth gathered plenty of food for her and her mother-in-law. But she also enjoyed the friendship and companionship of other women—fellowship during long days that could have very easily become lonely. In addition to all of that, she found herself under the protection and guidance of a kind, godly man who was a loving leader.

This was the best-case scenario for Ruth. Because despite the differences that may come to mind when we think of twelfth century BC versus twenty-first century AD, here's the big fat piece of cross-century, cross-generational common ground that almost all women share: we want to take really good care of our people. Ruth was able to do that.

And when we make our peace with the fact that we can only do what we can do—that we're not made to be all things to all people—we start to see how the Lord multiplies our efforts. Granted, most of us aren't working in a literal field like Naomi did, but we're still working in the metaphorical fields the Lord has given us: our families, our churches, our neighborhoods, our schools, our workplaces, our volunteer organizations. If we're mindful and faithful to glean a few minutes of margin from each day—the half-hour when we're driving our kids home from school, the forty-minute window between football practice drop-off and pick-up, the five minutes it takes to detour by a friend's house on the way home from work—we just may get to bear witness to the Lord providing supernatural abundance in the hearts and lives of the people we love.

Watch and see.

Isn't this the best news? We can all stop feeling like we have to present a hurting friend with Martha Stewart's cranberry wreath! We're wasting our time with all those broken toothpicks! So instead, maybe we just look for ten minutes in our day when we can stop by her house with some cranberries. Or oranges. Or any fruit rich in vitamin C. Hug her neck. Tell her that we love her. Pray with her.

BECAUSE RUTH IS OUR REMINDER THAT GOD RICHLY PROVIDES IN THE GLEANING.

Look at what my dear (pretend) friend Mary Elizabeth Baxter wrote back in the nineteenth century:

> Ruth did not assume to be a reaper, but ONLY A GLEANER. There are some prominent workers in the harvest field who sweep hundreds into the fold. But there are also patient gleaners who teach in Sunday schools, who visit from house to house, who write letters to their acquaintances, who speak a word to those they travel with by the way. God bless these precious gleaners. They gather many an ear of corn which reapers pass by (emphasis mine).[24]

And if we still need one more reminder—one more assurance—then we'd do well to sing the words from an old hymn by Kittie Suffield called "Little Is Much When God Is in It."

> *In the harvest field now ripened*
> *There's a work for all to do;*
> *Hark! the voice of God is calling,*
> *To the harvest calling you.*
>
> *Little is much when God is in it!*
> *Labor not for wealth or fame;*
> *There's a crown, and you can win it,*
> *If you go in Jesus' name.*

In the mad rush of the broad way,
In the hurry and the strife,
Tell of Jesus' love and mercy,
Give to them the Word of Life.
Does the place you're called to labor
Seem so small and little known?
It is great if God is in it,
And He'll not forget His own.[25]

Kittie knew what was up, y'all.
Glean on, my friends.
Glean on.

Chapter 9

It's Totally Fine to Point at Jesus

One of the kicky things about sitting here in the middle of my forties is that sometimes I find myself bogged down in what I like to call the "kids, get off my lawn" syndrome. It's not my consistent mind-set by any stretch of the imagination; keep in mind that I work with teenagers for a living and love that age group more than is even rational; I really do try to be a fairly objective observer of what's going on in their world even if I'm not always a participant.

Every once in a while, though, some cultural phenomenon with younger folks will strike me as so utterly ridiculous it makes me rant-y. And while I don't literally stand in my front yard while wearing a housecoat and sporting some sponge rollers in my hair—while I don't actually wave my arms around and yell at neighborhood kids to get off my property as I wield a stick or a cane or a full mug of coffee—my immediate emotional response to the annoying trend at hand falls somewhere along the lines of "TAKE YOUR SILLINESS SOMEWHERE ELSE, KIDS—I DON'T HAVE TIME FOR THIS NONSENSE."

So when a child star turned pop star performs on national television while dressed up like a mouse that can't seem to keep its tongue in its mouth?

GET OFF MY LAWN.

When a new music video goes viral despite the fact that it's loaded with way too many near-naked bodies and the song is full of mindless, sexist, misogynistic lyrics?

GET OFF MY LAWN.

(And also: THIS RECORDING ARTIST DOESN'T SEEM TO HAVE A VERY HIGH VIEW OF WOMEN.)

When the person in front of me in Starbucks holds up the line so that he and a buddy can Dubsmash a scene from *The Wolf of Wall Street*?

GET OFF MY LAWN—BUT NOT UNTIL I WASH YOUR MOUTH OUT WITH SOAP.

See? I am a sensitive, gentle soul.

I rarely vocalize these feelings because (1) the world already has plenty of self-righteousness, and (2) whether I like what's going on in pop culture or not, the lay of the land is the lay of the land, and if I want to continue to develop relationships with the generation behind me, I have to be able to speak their language to a certain extent.

And as a quick sidebar: their language? Thanks in no small part to the Kardashians? Sometimes involves saying a lot of sentences as questions? And also saying the word "thanks" as "thennnnnnnnks"?

This is merely an observation, not a judgment.

LOOK AT ME NOT JUDGING YOU, MILLENNIAL FRIENDS.

I really am smiling so big right now.

From time to time my mother-in-law, Martha, will give me instructions about something she'd like for me to do. It usually goes a little something like this.

"*Sophie? If you don't mind, sugar? Would you take this jacket back to the Stein Mart by your house? It's not that I don't love it—I do! I love it! I really do!—but the neck and shoulders are just cut way too big and fall down to HERE when I try to wear one of my mock turtlenecks underneath. But now that reminds me! If you see any mock turtlenecks when you go to return the jacket? Well, I would just love a royal blue one or a Kelly green one or a hot pink one. I have a red one and a navy one and a black one, but don't you think one of those brighter colors would be so pretty? Just for some POP underneath a jacket or a coat? I think they'd be so pretty! Really pretty! So that's all I need, sugar. Just to return the jacket. And maybe a few mock turtlenecks. And be sure to tell them that I love everything I get from there! It's my favorite store! It really is!*"

So maybe that's why, at the beginning of Ruth 3, I totally relate to the fact that Naomi is giving Ruth a few instructions. Granted, Naomi wasn't terribly concerned with 3/4-sleeve jackets or mock turtlenecks, but she definitely had a to-do list in mind for her daughter-in-law.

And she had her reasons.

Naomi knew that Boaz was a kinsman-redeemer for Elimelech's family, meaning that by law he could lift any shame or condemnation attached to a close family member who found themselves in difficult circumstances. Redemption typically happened one of three ways: (1) redeeming a family member being held in slavery, (2) redeeming land by purchasing it when a family member was going through a tough time financially, and/or (3) redeeming the family name by marrying a widowed relative.[26]

And since Naomi wanted the very best for Ruth—according to Ruth 3:1, she wanted to "seek rest for [her], that it may be well with [her]"—pointing Ruth in Boaz's direction meant that Naomi was pointing her daughter-in-law toward a better future. She was pointing her toward redemption.

Now.

Ruth was from Moab, which meant she wasn't necessarily familiar with Israel's redemption process, so Naomi gave her step-by-step instructions. And because lists make me happy, I will now share said instructions in a convenient numbered format. Please note that biblical content is bolded, lest you confuse my stream-of-consciousness rambling with the Word of God.

AS IF.

Okay. Here's Naomi's to-do list for Ruth.

1. **Wash up.** Such an important tip. Wise counsel from Naomi.
2. **Anoint yourself.** I think the gist of this one was "Put on some oil and get that skin looking right, Ruth."
3. **Put on your cloak.** Makes sense. My mama has always said that if you look your best, you'll feel your best.
4. **Go down to the threshing floor where Boaz is.** 10-4. Sort of like meeting him at work.
5. **Don't interrupt his mealtime.** #wisdom

6. **Stay hidden until he goes to sleep and make note of where he lies down.** Maybe a little strange, but, um, fair enough.
7. **After he lies down, uncover his feet and lie down, too.** Not gonna lie, Naomi. This is straight-up weird to me.
8. **Wait for him to tell you what to do next.** Sounds good. Maybe that will alleviate some of the inevitable awkward.

So yeah. The instructions were super-specific, and it can be tricky for us to understand the whys and wherefores. Israeli customs seem odd when there are a few thousand years between then and now, so we have to remember that Naomi knew the redemptive drill.

And fortunately, people way smarter than I can give this whole exchange some context:

> Naomi's care for her daughter's comfort is without doubt very commendable. . . . It is the duty of parents to seek [the rest of marriage] for their children, and to do all that is fit for them to do, in due time, in order to it. . . . [Naomi did this] in justice to the dead, to raise up seed to those that were gone, and . . . to preserve the family from being extinct.[27]

Here's something else to remember. Naomi had a voice in Ruth's life, which meant she had the freedom to counsel her and guide her. Naomi knew Ruth better than anyone else; at the point when Naomi told Ruth to visit Boaz, the two women had lived side-by-side for, what? Eleven years? Naomi knew Ruth's history, she knew who she was behind closed doors, and she knew, based on the way her daughter-in-law had cared for her, that Ruth was worthy of a man as fine and respected as Boaz.

We all need someone who knows us that well.

That level of familiarity breeds trust. And in Ruth 3:4, we see Ruth's reaction to Naomi's instructions: "All that you say I will do."

There was no second-guessing, no arguing, no defiance. Just one big "Yes, ma'am. You got it."

RUTH TRUSTED HER MOTHER-IN-LAW'S WISDOM, SHE TRUSTED HER PLAN FOR REDEMPTION, AND ULTIMATELY, SHE TRUSTED HER WITH HER FUTURE.

From that perspective, there was nothing to debate. So off Ruth went—down to Boaz's threshing floor.

About eight or nine years ago, I read an article about how an increasing number of teenagers were participating in something called "sexting." At the time I didn't even know what "sexting" was (hence the "air quotes"), but my initial reaction was *Oh my word—that's the dumbest thing I've ever heard.*

GET OFF MY LAWN.

It just seemed so, I don't know, *silly* to me. After all, when I was growing up, if one of my friends or I had wanted to send an inappropriate picture to someone, we'd first have to go to the drug store and buy a roll of film. Then, once we got to wherever we were planning to take the (hypothetical) pictures, we'd have to use the whole roll of film. (Here's a photography lesson for the kids: if you opened the back of a camera before you finished using all 24 or 36 exposures, the entire roll was ruined.) After we finished using the whole roll of film, we'd have to take it somewhere to get it developed—probably a drug store—and then wait about a week for the prints to come back from the lab. At that point getting the pictures *still* wouldn't be guaranteed, because the photo clerks would have called our mamas in a heartbeat if they saw pictures where we, for whatever reason, had neglected to wear our clothes.

Yes, OF COURSE, the pictures would have been a bad idea to begin with. But ultimately we would have had a week of buffer between the idea and the execution of it, with all manner of speed bumps and guardrails set up along the way.

These days, though, it's different. We live in an insta-society where we can snap a picture and send it to hundreds of people in a matter of seconds. That's all fine and good and convenient when you're at Disney World and want to send a quick update to the grandparents. It's not so good, though, when you're a fifteen-year-old girl holding your phone in front of the bathroom mirror and contemplating taking off your top for the cute guy in geometry who asked you to send him some nudes.

It's been about eight-ish years since I read the sexting article, and I now know that it's a very real problem. In fact, I'm a little surprised by how often I think about it. That's not because it's something I do—oh my word, no. I'm in my forties. I've never sexted in my life, and even if I decided that sexting my husband was a good idea, the raciest thing I'd be able to come up with is, "Hey. Will you pick up some Chick-fil-A salads on your way home from work?"

It's funny because it's true.

But I think I can get a little fixated on this one thing because I love the teenagers I serve, I know how tough it is for them to fight the battles that surround them, and I desperately want to be able to point at one specific issue they're facing and say, HEY, EVERYBODY. THIS IS IT. THIS IS THE BIG BAD THREAT. IF WE CAN FIX THIS, WE'RE GOOD.

Way down deep, though, I know that when it comes to the generation behind us, sexting really isn't the biggest problem. Neither is apathy, for that matter. Neither is smoking marijuana or battling an eating disorder or maintaining a carefully crafted illusion of perfection. They're all symptoms of the problem. But they're really not the great big honkin' problem.

Here's what I mean.

One night last week I decided to watch a movie a lot of my twenty-something friends have seen. By and large I do a pretty terrible job of keeping up with movies, but I wanted to see this particular comedy. It was one of last summer's big blockbusters, and it has come up in conversations over and over again.

So I settled in. I watched. And by the thirty-ish minute mark, I had come to the firm conclusion that it wasn't my kind of movie at all. Honestly, I was pretty offended. Sure, there had been a few funny moments, but mostly it just struck me as sad. My mama would say it was "tacky, coarse, and crude," but the bigger issue for me? The main character wasn't likable. I didn't know how to root for her. She seemed content to wallow in her bad choices and sabotage her relationships. She didn't seem to hold herself in very high regard—you could search all day long for her self-respect and never find it—so it was difficult for me to root for her.

GET OFF MY LAWN.

And yes. I know. THE MOVIE IS PRETEND. THIS UNLIKABLE CHARACTER IS NOT REAL. But stay with me because all of this totally applies to a way bigger point.

So.

About twenty minutes before the movie was over, there were two things that sparked some compassion and grabbed my attention. The first was a song playing in the background during a break-up sequence. You know how those things typically go: girl and guy call it quits, girl and guy are miserable, girl journals at a coffee shop, guy sits on a park bench. The plot point wasn't terribly original, but I thought the lyrics from a Wilco song were pretty insightful:

> *"I should warn you*
> *When I'm not well*
> *I can't tell*
> *Oh, there's nothing I can do*
> *To make this easier for you*
> *You're gonna need to be patient with me."*[28]

That was such a good, timely reminder. I get that it's sort of a *strange* reminder in a somewhat unusual context, but my frustration with that movie character was no different than occasional frustrations with my high school kids or with my own family members: I fall into the trap of just wanting people to behave instead of loving them right where they are. I forget that none of us have ever been bossed into sincere repentance and life-changing redemption. Grace doesn't work that way.

So that was the first spark. Here's the second.

After the break-up sequence, the character who had been on my nerves throughout the whole movie goes to her sister's house. They had a big falling out at their father's funeral, so they hadn't talked in a while. And as the sister sits and stares, stiff-backed and skeptical, the main character gets as honest as we've seen her:

"I'm sorry. I'm really sorry . . . I'm not okay. I'm not okay. I know what I am. I know who I am. And I'm broken."

THERE IT IS.

As the kids like to say: *YASSSSSSSSSS.*

Because that's it, isn't it? That's the great big honkin' problem.

WE ARE ALL SO BROKEN.

Brokenness is going to manifest itself in thousands of different ways. I certainly won't attempt to put together a comprehensive list, but for the sake of discussion, I'll mention a few: we're unloving, we're unforgiving, we're self-sabotaging, we're insecure, we're bitter, we're hyper-judgmental, we're self-harming, we're addicted, we're dishonest, and we're desperate for someone to validate us via sexting, hook-ups, or porn.

The world takes a toll, y'all. Combine that with our sin, and it can be a no bueno situation.

So this is why, older believers, we have to come alongside our younger folks in the most patient, loving, truthful, and understanding ways. This is why we have to intentionally build relationships (even with our own kids—because sharing square footage isn't the same thing as living in community), why we have to be in it for the long haul, and why we can't just clasp our pearls in feigned outrage when a teenager tells us that they're getting wasted at least three nights a week or a twenty-something friend tells us that she "accidentally" slept with a guy she met in a bar.

And by the same token, this is why those of us in our thirties, forties, and fifties need to make sure that there's an older woman (or two) who knows what's really going on in our lives. Our issues may not be exactly what we see younger women facing (or who knows—they may be), but I think we all know that age doesn't offer immunity from struggles and shame.

Admitting our brokenness is yuck. Coming to terms with it is humbling. But no matter how our brokenness has manifested itself—no matter how it's holding us—it's good to remember that we have a Redeemer who faithfully frees us from condemnation, who continually shatters the lies of our counterfeit gods, who graciously ushers us out of darkness and covers us with Marvelous Light.

That's Good News.

And the younger women in our lives need to hear it.

I hope you know, by the way, that I'm not trying to be bossy. Not at all. I'm just saying, *Hey, older people. There's a generation behind us that needs us. So what's the plan? Are we going to stick our heads in the sand? Or are we going to fight for the hearts and minds of the folks who may require a little extra patience right now?*

Because I don't know about you, but this is one instance where I don't want the kids to get off my lawn.

I want them to stay on my lawn. In fact, I want them to sit a spell.

And I want to talk about some things.

So Boaz, I'm guessing, must have been all kinds of confused.

The harvest season was busy, and he'd worked late winnowing the barley. Afterward he'd enjoyed a great meal. According to Scripture, in fact, "his heart was merry." However, he was no doubt tired after a long day, so he stretched out on a pile of grain, closed his eyes, and went to sleep.

But at midnight he woke up to find that there was a woman laying at his feet.

Apparently Ruth had followed Naomi's instructions to the letter.

Boaz, no doubt startled by the presence of an unexpected visitor, asked what I think any of us would: "Who are you?"

I'd be willing to bet that Ruth's heart was beating a mile a minute. I mean, how do you even begin to explain who you are? Why you're there? What are you doing sleeping at a man's feet when he's made himself a bed on a heap of grain?

But Ruth was characteristically straightforward in her answer. "I am Ruth, your servant. Spread your wings over your servant, for you are a redeemer" (Ruth 3:9).

No kidding—this part of the story makes me want to put my hands over my eyes (and my ears) and rock back and forth a little bit, because Ruth made herself so incredibly vulnerable in that moment. She essentially asked Boaz to be her covering—to take her as his wife—and there's a part of me (a part that apparently has some deep-seated rejection issues) that wants to say, "Nooooooo, sister! Don't do it! Don't volunteer for that much vulnerability! This could turn out very badly!"

Boaz, however, was as kind and gracious as you'd expect a redeemer to be. The first words out of his mouth were "May you be blessed by the LORD, my daughter" (v. 10)—and then he offered

Ruth as much assurance as he possibly could. He esteemed her conduct, he told her not to be afraid, he validated her as "a worthy woman" (v. 11), and he shot straight with her about the possibility of "a redeemer nearer than I" (v. 12). Boaz knew that another relative of Mahlon and Elimelech—a man with a closer kinship—might ultimately be Ruth's redeemer. But even in the midst of that uncertainty, Boaz treated Ruth with enormous respect.

He also left zero room for doubt or confusion (oh, I *do* like a decisive, plain-spoken man). In verse 13, he said, "Remain tonight, and in the morning, if [the other relative] will redeem you, go; let him do it. But if he is not willing to redeem you, then, as the LORD lives, I will redeem you. Lie down until the morning."

Ruth knew exactly where she stood with him before she went to sleep. On top of that, by not sending her out into the night, Boaz made sure she was safe and had an opportunity to rest. There weren't any overtures, there wasn't any compromise, and because of that, there wouldn't be any regret or shame, either.

This is what good men do, by the way. They honor women. They look out for women. And they don't play games.

Before Ruth went home the next morning, Boaz gave her "six measures of barley" (v. 15) which, in modern measurements, officially amounts to A LOT. It was "as much as she could well carry,"[29] and when Ruth finally saw Naomi (who must have been on pins and needles waiting to hear about the night), she told her what had happened, including what we assume were Boaz's parting words: "You must not go back empty-handed to your mother-in-law."

(Hey—there's a good Life Tip for you: good men don't leave you and your people empty-handed.)

(And for that matter, a redeemer will never leave you empty-hearted.)

(Why do I suddenly feel the need to snap? What's wrong with me?)

Boaz definitely provided for Naomi's and Ruth's physical needs with that big barley haul. But there's something else going on, too; Naomi's final words in chapter 3 indicated that she trusted Boaz's ability to provide in other ways. She told Ruth, "'Wait, my daughter, until you learn how the matter turns out, for the man will not rest but will settle the matter today'" (v. 18).

Isn't it interesting? At the beginning of Ruth 3, Naomi told Ruth she wanted to "seek rest" for her. Then Ruth went to see Boaz, and he told her to "lie down," essentially giving her the gift of rest when she could have worried and paced all night. And later, in verse 18, Naomi told Ruth to "wait"—to take it easy—because Boaz would *not* rest until he followed through on his word.

Ruth endured the death of her first husband. She traveled to a new country. She lived as a foreigner in a strange land. She battled poverty. She labored in the fields. She faced unfamiliar customs. But after her kinsman-redeemer entered the picture—she could rest. She could wait. She could breathe.

And all of this was possible because of the companionship, counsel, and wisdom of her mother-in-law.

Think about that for a second. Yes, Naomi needed Ruth for the journey back to Bethlehem. But I'm confident that Ruth needed Naomi just as much. How else would she have known about the wonder, the promise, and the peace of redemption?

Those two paths were meant to intersect.

And those two lives can teach us.

This life is a gift—no doubt about it—but it is not for the faint of heart. Navigating the journey can be tough, and we're bound to trip up from time to time. Odds are we'll also make a few wrong turns. So if we've been walking the road a little longer—if we're more familiar with the terrain—it is right and good for us to extend a hand to a younger friend or relative who isn't quite as sure which way to go. We can carry an extra bag or two. We can even share some directions when the route gets confusing.

But more than anything else, as we travel together—as we start and stop and lead and follow and rest and start again—we can lovingly, consistently, and patiently point each other toward the Light, our heavenly Father, our Eternal Redeemer.

It may not be an easy road, but it's the path of peace.

And it's the only Way that leads us Home.

Chapter 10

We May Have to Walk Uphill Together, but at Least It's Good for Our Calves

"I should probably tell you," my friend Keely said as she leaned across the aisle, "that the landing is sort of tricky."

At the time we were about forty-five minutes away from our destination of Quito, Ecuador, and Keely and I—along with the rest of our Compassion International travel group—were on a flight where the people and the bags and the stuff and the things were so jammed and wedged and piled into the seats and overhead bins there wasn't a centimeter of room for anything else, not even so much as a Barbie doll's purse. I personally was teetering right on the edge of THIS PLANE IS SO CROWDED THAT I MAY NEED TO CRY, which meant that Keely's words felt like an additional shock to my already overloaded nervous system.

In the moment I had no idea how to respond, so I leaned back in my seat, closed my eyes, and tried to block out the swirl of conversations around me. I don't mind flying—in fact, I actually love to travel—but considering that I was about to hit my limit of in-flight togetherness, I wasn't quite ready to deal with the not-so-small matter of coping with, you know, *imminent scary landing danger.*

Clearly I was in a very rational state of mind.

For the duration of our flight, I prayed and I prayed and I prayed. I don't really remember the specifics of what I prayed, but I would not be at all surprised to know that I pulled out some of the more obscure names of God because TERRIFIED.

I mean, I can't really think of another instance when I've felt led to call on "Jehovah Metshodhathi," but if there were ever a time, it was right then and there.

Now I don't know what happened—if the pilot took an alternate route into Quito, if my expectations were so out of kilter that reality paled in comparison, if a couple of penguins took a cue from *Madagascar 2* and turned the plane into a parachute before they set it down gently on the runway—but the landing wasn't nearly as bad as I feared. So by the time we deplaned, made our way through security, pulled our luggage from baggage claim, and walked out to the bus that was waiting for us (and I don't mean to brag, but I WAS ALIVE FOR ALL OF IT), I may have been feeling a little smug.

Oh, Ecuador, I thought, *you are going to be a piece of cake!*

Oh, Ecuador, I thought, *we are going to have many wonderful, meaningful moments together!*

Oh, Ecuador, I thought, *we got off to a rough start because of that jam-packed flight, but this is a reset button! Never mind the diesel fumes, Ecuador—we are going to be just fine!*

However, if Ecuador could have laughed at me in that moment, I feel certain she would have. Because Ecuador was holding a couple of secrets up her sleeve.

And the first one was the altitude.

Now I recognize, of course, that some of you more seasoned (or organized) travelers would have anticipated the altitude from the very day you decided to go to Ecuador, but I, for whatever reason, failed to consider the full effects of traveling from Birmingham, which is roughly 600 feet above sea level, to Quito, which is over 9,000 feet above sea level.

Oh, I figured I might be a little short of breath, but by 8:00 the morning after our arrival, I knew beyond a shadow of a doubt that the altitude differential, it did not play. I was flushed, I was nauseated, my head was pounding, and whenever I tried to do anything that required me to, oh, STAND UP, I'd inevitably look over at my friend and roommate Melanie and say, "I'm gonna need to lie down for a couple more seconds" before I face-planted on the bed. It was like somebody had filled my arms and legs with lead while I was sleeping, and just getting dressed felt like an act of courage. Eventually, though, Melanie and I walked down to breakfast in the hotel lobby, and I think it was Keely who said, "You need caffeine ASAP, and then you need so much water. SO VERY MUCH WATER. You need ALL THE WATER."

I took Keely's advice to heart, and within fifteen minutes I knew my newly formed relationship with Ecuadoran coffee would remain precious to me for the rest of my earthly days. Sure, we had just met, but from the get-go it treated me so right. Between the coffee and the water, I was a semi-normal person when we boarded our bus about forty-five minutes later, and I was excited about spending the day with some Compassion families in a city about an hour and a half away.

Unfortunately, that bus ride is when Ecuador revealed her second secret: curvy mountain roads.

The word "curvy" has never been more of an understatement, by the way. I can't even think of an adjective that would do those roads justice.

Spiral?

Corkscrew?

Mind-numbingly precarious?

I'll keep thinking.

In the meantime, suffice it to say that the curving was significant.

I was fine as we drove through Quito's downtown area, but as soon as we started our ascent up the mountain, the combination of an un-air-conditioned bus, strong diesel fumes, and hairpin turns started to do a number on me. For several miles I tried to fight the queasiness with mind over matter, but about the time my mind would cooperate, that bus would shift gears and we'd make another turn.

After twenty or so minutes, I glanced in my friend Kelly's direction and said, "Um, I'm not feeling so hot. Are you feeling like I'm feeling?"

Kelly's face was sort of a yellow-ish green. So I took that as a yes.

About that time Keely, our resident travel expert and our trip photographer, jumped into action. "Girls! You need some crackers or chips! We have a whole bag full—hold on just a minute. And just so you know—if you turn around in your seat to talk, it makes the nausea worse. Look outside the front window as much as you can, and you'll be surprised how much it helps."

Within seconds there was a plastic bag on my seat with all manner of Ecuadoran snack foods inside. I pulled out some corn chips and Kelly opted for the local version of Doritos called "Mega Queso."

I felt like she made a good choice. There's not a whole lot in life that Big Cheese can't fix.

The corn chips weren't my favorite—they tasted much more like actual corn than our corn chips in America, and apparently "natural flavor" isn't what I'm looking for in my snack products— so I set them aside and closed my eyes again. I could hear my friends Ann and Patricia sitting behind me, carrying on a very thoughtful conversation about, oh, I don't know, general revelation vs. special revelation; meanwhile I was doing my level best to lift my head long enough to look at Kelly and say, "Can I haz uno Dorito so maybe no vomit?"

So I guess you could say that Ecuador and I, we were off to a slow start.

But if the way our bus was bookin' it around those curves was any indication, we'd be picking up speed in no time.

For the last month or so the soundtrack from a well-known Broadway musical has been on steady rotation in my iTunes. Usually I'm not a huge fan of a musical, but this particular show has created an exception to the rule. It's a history lesson in a way I've never heard it taught, and the level of creativity in the writing and the performing is crazy inspiring.

Since the musical has been playing in the background a good bit as I've been writing about Ruth, Naomi, and Boaz, I've decided that if there were such a thing as *Ruth: The Musical* (or *Ruth! The Musical)*, the first act—after all the men's deaths, Ruth's sacrificial willingness to follow her mother-in-law to a strange land, and Naomi's insistence that her friends call her "Mara" because the Lord had dealt bitterly with her—would more than likely conclude with a monotone song in a minor key. And the chorus, I imagine, would primarily involve a lot of really loud weeping and wailing.

But as we know, the story takes a more hopeful turn after Ruth 1, and by Ruth 4, things are moving full speed ahead. Boaz went to the city gate after Ruth left the threshing floor, and while he was there, the other relative / potential redeemer "happened" to walk by. Boaz, who seemed to subscribe to the GET 'ER DONE school of handling personal affairs, asked the relative to sit down. He also gathered ten elders to serve as witnesses, and once everybody was seated and settled, Boaz started to break down the Ruth/ Naomi situation.

(I'll summarize.)

(I so wish I knew how to rap right now.)

(I guess the Mississippi translation of this part of Ruth 4 will have to do.)

So everybody was sitting down, and since he was super smart, Boaz explained the circumstances in the most laid-back fashion. He looked over at the other possible redeemer and said, "Hey. Naomi is back from Moab, and she wants to sell the land that belonged to Elimelech. I thought you might want to know, because if you want to buy it, you can agree to that in front of these witnesses I've pulled together. It's yours for the taking. But if you don't want to buy it, you need to let me know, because I'm next in line, and I'd like to buy it if you don't."

The relative said, "Okay, then. I'll buy it."

What the relative didn't know, however, was that Boaz had a trump card, and that trump card was named Ruth.

So Boaz—in the most oh-did-I-forget-to-mention-this-part way—said, "Perfect. Great. But there are a couple more pieces to this puzzle."

You know he had the relative's complete attention in that moment.

"If you buy the land, you're also responsible for marrying Ruth, the Moabite widow of one of Elimelech's sons. So you'll have to be her husband, and then of course part of your redeemer responsibility will be to have some young'uns with Ruth in order to carry on the family name."

Those last two things seemed to give the relative pause. Somehow, I think, Boaz knew that they would.

So even though he'd been all in when it was just land at stake, the relative wasn't interested in any relational commitments. He said, "Nope. No can do. I'm out. I can't have more kids since that will jeopardize the inheritance of the kids I already have."

And then, at what would no doubt be the moment in *Ruth! The Musical* when the orchestra music would start to swell, the relative looked at Boaz and said, "It's all yours. The land. Ruth. The future young'uns. REDEEM AWAY, my friend. And to seal this arrangement, I will now take off my shoe and offer it to you."

Because that was a real thing, you know. The shoe was sort of like a signature—only it was made of leather and considerably smellier than any signature has ever thought about being.

Nonetheless, between the shoe and the presence of the witnesses, Boaz's right of redemption was officially official.

So Boaz, being a stand-up guy, addressed the elders, along with the other folks who had gathered at the city gate, and officially announced his intentions to buy Elimelech's land and marry Ruth. It was what he had wanted all along. I can't help but think that if Ruth and Naomi were listening off to the side somewhere, they probably high-fived. Maybe even fist-bumped with a little explosion motion.

And you know what I may love more than anything else in this first half of Ruth 4? The elders affirmed Boaz and Ruth right there at the city gate. By now y'all probably know that I think it's important for the body of believers to BLESS SOME PEOPLE as they walk out what the Lord is calling them to do, and that's exactly how the folks who witnessed Boaz's proclamation responded.

> We are witnesses. May the LORD make the woman, who is coming into your house, like Rachel and Leah, who together built up the house of Israel. May you act worthily in Ephrathah and be renowned in Bethlehem, and may your house be like the house of Perez, whom Tamar bore to Judah, because of the offspring that the LORD will give you by this young woman. (vv. 11–12)

David Guzik frames the confirmation and blessing of Boaz's redemption this way: "Back in chapter one, Ruth seemed to be giving up on her best chance of marriage by leaving her native land of Moab and giving her heart and life to the God of Israel. But as Ruth put God first, He brought her together in a relationship greater than she could have imagined."[30]

The Lord is always in the business of working out a new and better thing, isn't He?

Always.

No matter where we traveled in Ecuador, those curvy roads were a constant. The third day, in fact, I met Wilter, one of the kids my family and I sponsor through Compassion. He and his mom, Marta, actually hopped on the bus with us (you'd better believe I'd taken two Dramamine at breakfast; LESSON LEARNED, Ecuador). I was super tired that morning, and honestly, I was a little concerned about spending the day with a family I'd never met. I didn't want anyone to feel awkward or unwelcome, but I wondered how in the world I was going to talk and interact for a full day when all I really wanted was sleep. However, the other girls on the trip cheered me on and assured me that they would jump in and help if I ran out of conversation topics or had a momentary run-in with nausea.

It never occurred to any of us, though, that Wilter, who lives in a coastal area of Ecuador, probably wasn't used to Quito's altitude, much less riding on a bus in the mountains. He would nervously grab the seat in front of him whenever the bus made a sharp turn, so I tried talk to him and his mom in my very broken Spanish and hopefully put them both at ease. About ten minutes before we arrived at the church we were visiting, though, I noticed that he was extra quiet. As soon as we reached our destination and walked off the bus, I learned the real story behind that silence.

Let me put it this way: maybe a package of Mega Queso Doritos could have cured what ailed Wilter. But in the absence of those Doritos, Wilter reached the bottom of the bus steps and lost his battle with motion sickness in the most (literally) gut-wrenching way. I felt so sorry for him. However, since he was an eight-year-old boy, he got sick, took a minute to regroup, and then started running through the grass, pointing at the sky and yelling at the sight of an airplane.

And throughout the morning, the other women on the trip—who for sure shared my displaced and loopy and mildly nauseated feelings—continually checked on Wilter and his mama. They kicked around the soccer ball, they struck up conversations, and they basically helped me feel like a whole, functioning person.

Some days, I guess, it takes seven other people to do that.

Well.

A few hours after Wilter's run-in with travel-related nausea, I did my best to carry on a conversation in Spanish with Marta. I managed to use the correct Spanish to ask if she liked to cook, and when she said yes, I asked what kinds of foods were Wilter's favorites. She rattled off a list of foods that sounded mostly unfamiliar to me, but there was a point when I heard two magical words: *pollo frito.*

Fried chicken.

It really is a universal love language.

I got so excited by our common culinary ground that I quickly looked at Wilter and said, "I LOVE FRIED CHICKEN!" in Spanish. In my haste, however, I apparently mixed up a couple of reflexive verbs, because about the time I started trying to figure out why Wilter looked so confused by my adoration for fried chicken, my friend Amanda leaned over and said, "Um, Sophie? I'm pretty sure that you just told Wilter that your name is fried chicken."

To this day I'm grateful that Amanda was keeping close enough tabs on us that she was able to correct my mistake. And really, that is just one example of my effectiveness in an international ministry context. Feel free to e-mail me if you'd like more tips and suggestions about lasting missional impact, my friends.

Skills. I've got 'em.

Not too long after I unintentionally renamed myself, we got back on the bus, and after one final stop, headed back to the hotel. I don't know that Wilter enjoyed the winding roads any more than he had when we made the first leg of the trip, but his whole demeanor was different. Instead of clutching the back of the seat, he looked relaxed, leaned against my shoulder, and fell sound asleep. I guess sometimes those curvy roads get a little easier the second time around, especially if we've come to trust our fellow travelers. And after we eventually made it back to our hotel, I was sad to say good-bye to Wilter and Marta before they began their return trip home.

The next morning, our team returned to the bus (are you noticing a pattern?) for our longest journey yet: a five-hour trip to the Amazon jungle. The plan was to travel to the very top of Mega Queso Mountain (to be clear, I don't think this is the *official* name of that particular landmark)—12,000 feet above sea level—and then make our descent to the jungle on the other side. Of all the things we did on the trip, I was the most nervous about the Amazon part; even getting on the bus that morning felt like someone was holding a giant megaphone in front of my face and screaming, "NOW IT IS TIME TO ABANDON YOUR COMFORT ZONE."

I settled into my seat, took another Dramamine for good measure, and closed my eyes. Before I knew it, I dozed off, and y'all, it was about an hour and a half later when I woke up. After I got my bearings (bus, mountain, Ecuador—got it), I looked out my window. We weren't quite to the top of the mountain, but we were close, and we were on a road that seemed about as wide as the skinny gold belt I used to wear with my green Gloria Vanderbilt corduroys back in my elementary school days. For several miles I was hyper-aware that a wrong turn or a severe swerve would be Very Bad News Indeed, and the part of my mind and heart that likes to control and plan and dictate was feeling pretty anxious. Our driver whipped around turns so fast I felt like I was at Talladega—to the point that I kind of wanted to put on some cutoff shorts and a tank top and climb on someone's shoulders—only my mood wasn't quite festive enough for a NASCAR race.

Somewhere in the middle of all my worry and my doubt, however, I realized we were surrounded by almost unimaginable beauty. Clouds dusted the tops of lush green mountains that seemed to stretch out in every direction. Way off in the distance, in the very highest areas, snow-capped peaks sat proudly like arrows pointing at the sky.

I didn't belong there. But somehow I did.

Keely mentioned that there was a waterfall off to our right, and as everybody spotted it—not to mention the spectacular scenery that surrounded it—our group started to sound like a chorus of older Southern women.

"Have you ever?"

"*I just cannot believe . . .*"
"*Is that not the most beautiful thing you've . . .*"
"*Well, my goodness!*"

And somewhere in the middle of Mountain Appreciation 101, the sound of my friends' voices reminded me that whether I liked traveling over that mountain or not—whether I was *comfortable* traveling it or not—those curvy, sometimes downright scary roads were affording us some once-in-a-lifetime views. They were giving us a unique perspective of God's goodness here on earth and showing us how He reveals Himself through His creation.

Those curvy roads? So worth it.

Plus, they ultimately led to the Amazon—which, as I was about to learn, is jaw-droppingly beautiful even if it's sort of an overachiever when it comes to heat and also bugs.

They were worth it.

Because even when we're uncertain, God holds.

He sustains.

He delivers.

And He gives us people who can point out what we may not always see.

Ruth and Naomi's situation looked pretty bleak in Ruth 1.

They had no idea what would be waiting on them when they arrived in Bethlehem, what with both of them being widowed, one spending over ten years in exile, and one being a Moabite.

But in the most wondrously unforeseen ways, the Lord foreshadowed future gospel glory through the stories of Naomi, Ruth, and Boaz. Boaz covered and redeemed Ruth; he removed the shame of Ruth's past and secured her inheritance. He took her as his bride.

Just that alone would have been a perfect ending, right? I mean, you could take that whole narrative and write a script and make a movie that would reduce Nicholas Sparks to tears. It's a beautiful love story.

The Lord, though, had an even bigger story to tell. Ruth and Boaz had a son named Obed, and Obed eventually fathered Jesse. Jesse had several sons, and one of them—a shepherd boy named David—was crowned as king. We've already seen how that played out in Luke 1 when Gabriel visited Mary: "[Your son] will be great and will be called the Son of the Most High. And the Lord God will give to him the throne of his father David, and he will reign over the house of Jacob forever, and of his kingdom there will be no end" (vv. 32–33).

Ruth didn't just make a way for Naomi to get home. She made a way for Jesus.

It was a shocking turn of events. A Moabite woman named Ruth—a woman who had been widowed, childless, and poor, who was only in Bethlehem because of sacrificial loyalty to her mother-in-law—became the great-grandmother of King David. That family line eventually extended all the way to Mary, the mother of Jesus. It's astounding. According to Dr. David Platt, "God used a Moabite woman as a result of an Israelite who turned his back on the promised land to bring hope to an otherwise hopeless Israelite situation so that we would have the greatest King we know."[31]

And don't miss this, either: in the midst of the joys of Ruth and Boaz's redemptive story, Naomi was certainly not left out of the celebration. As a matter of fact, I think she probably experienced the biggest transformation of all. She was in a bad place when she traveled home from Moab; in Ruth 1, she said, "I went away full and the LORD has brought me back empty. Why call me Naomi, when the LORD has testified against me and the Almighty has brought calamity upon me?" (vv. 21–22).

But by the end of chapter 4, Naomi sang a different song. After the birth of her grandson, her friends gathered around her and said, "Blessed be the LORD, who has not left you this day without a redeemer, and may his name be renowned in Israel! He shall be to you a restorer of life and a nourisher of your old age, for your daughter-in-law who loves you, who is more to you than seven sons, has given birth to him" (vv. 14–15).

Obed secured Naomi's redemption just as Boaz had done for Ruth.

After everything Naomi had endured, she was full again. She laid that grandbaby on her lap, and while Scripture doesn't tell us exactly how long she held him, my guess is that Ruth probably had to beg a time or three to get that little man back in her arms.

Naomi's road wasn't easy. But I imagine she'd walk it a hundred times over knowing that Ruth, Boaz, and Obed were at the end of it.

As we close out this section, I want to point out five quick things that have occurred to me as we've talked about these four chapters. I hope these will be helpful as we think about our friendships across generations, but if they're not, just nod politely and maybe write down your own and this will all be over soon enough.

1. **Ruth let Naomi feel all her feelings.** There may have been a point when Ruth wanted to look at Naomi and say, "Hey, NayNay—LIGHTEN UP." But she didn't. She respected that the older woman's frame of mind was what it was, and she didn't try to change it / talk Naomi out of it / fix everything. She met her mother-in-law in the middle of her circumstances and loved her right there.

2. **Ruth's mentor / mother figure wasn't a stranger.** I know that we're big on finding mentors outside of our families, and that's great. I also know that we're big on mentoring younger people outside of our families, and that's great, too. Sometimes we live far from our people of origin and need folks in our communities to fill the gaps. But the person who might most need your loving care and attention—or who might best provide it for you—could very well be hanging out on a limb of your family tree. Stranger things have happened.

3. **Ruth and Naomi shared an enormous level of trust.** This one can be so hard, and it's why deep relational investment is so critical. We don't listen to people we don't trust. We don't get a voice with people who don't trust us. And trust is precisely why, when Naomi told Ruth to go lay at Boaz's feet after he fell asleep, Ruth's reaction was something along the lines of *Sure thing. Got it. Check.* She didn't question Naomi's methods because she trusted her motives. It's a good reminder that relational integrity matters. We must "guard [our] mouth with a muzzle" (Ps. 39:1)—not just in terms of keeping confidences, but also in terms of how we react

to one another and speak to one another. If someone consistently belittles or berates you, that person isn't a mentor. She certainly isn't a friend. She's a bully.

4. **The right way is the right way.** Ruth followed harvesting/gleaning protocol when she worked in the fields. She wasn't looking for special treatment and was content to do her work whether anyone noticed her or not. Then, when Naomi instructed Ruth about going to the threshing floor, she explained the right way to approach Boaz, the way that fell in line with the day's cultural practices. She didn't ask Ruth to do anything that would damage her reputation or cause Boaz to question her character. And finally, when Boaz met with the other potential redeemer, he handled the matter of redemption promptly, fairly, and openly. He did the right thing, and he did it the right way. So did Naomi. So did Ruth. They could all move forward without being tempted to look back.

5. **Ruth and Naomi's story was bigger than they could have ever expected.** When Ruth and Naomi walked from Moab to Bethlehem, I doubt that one of them piped up and said, "You know what? I bet people will read about us one day. I bet people will hold us up as the poster children for healthy in-law relationships. And you know what else? I bet somehow one of us will wind up in the family line of THE SAVIOR OF THE WHOLE WORLD." What a reminder that we don't get to design or control how the Lord intends to use our stories, and oh have mercy He will sure enough use them in ways that would never occur to us.

LOVE EACH OTHER WELL. TEND TO EACH OTHER WELL. WALK THIS THING OUT WITH EACH OTHER REALLY, REALLY WELL.

Ruth and Naomi didn't ride buses back in their time, because, well, there were no buses (please let me know if you'd like for me to point out any other incredibly obvious historical facts). But they knew a little something about navigating changes in elevation, about traveling over and through and around tricky terrain, about dealing with the exhaustion that settles in after a long and arduous journey. They'd made the descent out of Moab, walked down to a spot where the Jordan fed into the Dead Sea, crossed the river, and then had to finish the final leg of their trip by walking uphill to reach Bethlehem's elevation of roughly 2,500 feet above sea level.

And here's one more reminder from Captain Obvious: that path wasn't a straight line, and not one bit of it was paved.

But there were two constants during every step of their trek from exile to deliverance: (1) the ever-loving, ever-faithful hand of God, and (2) the encouragement and support they provided for each other.

They had no idea when they were in the middle of the journey, but ultimately they were instrumental in helping each other get where God wanted them to go. They were examples of "seemingly unimportant people at apparently insignificant times which later prove to be monumentally crucial to accomplishing God's will."[32]

As renowned biblical scholars might say, that's pretty cool, isn't it?

Get out there and walk out this thing with some people, y'all. You were made for it.

Lois and Eunice

Chapter 11

Teach Me Your Ways, Mamaw

When my mama was a little girl, her parents built a house on some farmland in south Mississippi. For over forty years they grew all kinds of vegetables, tended cows, raised chickens, and, more than anything else, created a haven for their children and grandchildren. As one of those grandchildren, I can tell you without hesitation that there isn't any place on earth that holds sweeter memories for me.

I think I was in the fourth grade when Mamaw and Papaw decided to sell the farm. It became more than they could manage, so they bought a house "in town" (if you consider a community with three stop signs a town, that is). We all missed the farm like crazy, and when a fire destroyed the old farmhouse several years later, we grieved. I was barely a teenager when it happened, and even though Mamaw and Papaw didn't live there anymore, it felt like the end of an era.

It's now been over thirty years since Mamaw and Papaw's old house burned. It's been almost forty years since our family had any claim to that land. But I don't think a single week passes when I don't talk about wanting to buy a tiny little piece of what used to be my grandparents' farm in Moss Rose, Mississippi. I can't really explain it, but my soul craves that place. My sister and my cousin Paige feel the same way.

And about three years ago, after a way-too-long separation, I felt like I needed to see that land again.

Alex and I were in my hometown visiting my parents over President's Day weekend, and that Monday morning I announced that it was high time for an impromptu family field trip. Mamaw and Papaw's old place wasn't that far away, and in addition to the fact that I had a personal pilgrimage on the brain, I really wanted Alex, who was ten, to finally see the place he'd heard about so often. He'd been listening to me talk about Mamaw and Papaw Davis—who both passed away before I graduated from high school—for his whole life, and it was high time for him to have a place to put with the people.

So Mama, Alex, and I climbed in my car, and off we went. It only took us about five minutes to get to the interstate, so I turned south, set the cruise control, and silently wondered how many times I'd sat in the back seat just like Alex while my daddy drove our family to Mamaw and Papaw's house.

I never did come up with a number. But we went at least once a month for the first twelve years of my life, so have at it, math geniuses.

After about twenty minutes we turned off the interstate onto the highway that leads to Moss Rose, and I later told my sister that as soon as we turned on that two-lane road, Mama was fifteen years old all over again. She narrated nonstop, telling us who lived where when she was a little girl, what they did for a living, whether they went to the Methodist or the Baptist church. Before too long we came to an intersection that used to have a blinking light but now has a stop sign, and instead of turning in the direction of Mamaw and Papaw's house, I went straight. Our first stop was going to be Moss Rose United Methodist Church.

Mama, a lifelong Methodist, grew up at Moss Rose UMC just like four generations of Davises before her. It's where she was baptized, where she first sang in the choir, and where she ate many a fried chicken leg at who knows how many dinners on the grounds. It's where she learned about Jesus, where she and Daddy were married, and where our family celebrated the lives of my grandparents when they went home to be with the Lord. Mama could always count on an abundance of aunts and uncles and cousins being in attendance—Moss Rose was chock-full-o-kinfolk—so every Sunday was like a family reunion. In fact, one of Mama's aunts, Myrtle, lived in a house about five steps away from the church—so close, in fact, that if she ever overslept for Sunday school, it would have been perfectly feasible for someone to open the church's front door, stand on the stoop, and yell, "HEY, MYRT—TIME TO WAKE UP!"

As far as I know, that never happened. But I bet you a dollar to a doughnut that Aunt Myrt kept track of the comings and goings in the church parking lot. I imagine she even called a few folks on her avocado rotary dial phone to let them know what was going on, too.

On the day of our visit, Mama, Alex, and I parked the car and walked around the church a bit, even tried to open a couple of doors. But when it was clear that we weren't going to be able to get in the sanctuary, we snapped a few pictures, got back in the car, and made a quick stop at the cemetery before we finally found what used to be Mamaw and Papaw's driveway. The current owner of the property put up a fence running the length of what used be the front yard and the most visible section of the pasture, so Alex and I would have to climb over a gate if we wanted to do any exploring.

We most definitely wanted to explore. And since Mama could name almost every family who lives in that neck of the woods— and since no one actually lives on Mamaw and Papaw's land anymore—we felt like it was okay to do a tiny bit of trespassing.

So that is exactly what we did.

Mama opted to stay in the car since fence-climbing wasn't too high on her list, and as soon as Alex and I climbed the fence and stepped onto what used to be Mamaw and Papaw's driveway, I felt a lump form in the back of my throat. While I had expected that standing on that land might cause a few memories to flutter across my mind, I wasn't prepared for how they washed over me—and with some authority, at that.

We stood in silence for a minute, my boy and me, while I let my eyes roam from one side of the property to the other. Then I took a deep breath, grabbed Alex's hand, and started walking.

Part of Mamaw and Papaw's chimney survived the fire (plus the thirty years since), and the first thing I noticed as we walked toward it was the cast iron cleanout door on the front. I must have opened and closed that thing a thousand times over the course of my childhood; it used to squeak like crazy, and sometimes I'd even scoop out the ashes. It was hanging by one hinge, so I didn't touch it, but even the sight of it made me feel like I'd traveled back in time. My attention gradually shifted to the concrete steps that used to lead to the front door; how in the world they were still standing was beyond me. I wondered if they'd still make a good stage for a pretend Miss America evening gown competition. Heaven knows they served pretty well in that capacity when I was younger.

The buildings that surrounded the area where the house used to be were still standing and mostly intact. Papaw had built them all—a chicken coop, a smokehouse that later functioned as a workshop, a big barn with stables and a hayloft—and it flat-out delighted me for Alex to see the work of his great-grandfather's hands. We walked the perimeter of those buildings for ten minutes, probably, though it might be more accurate to say that what I actually did was wade in a deep river of nostalgia. I rubbed my hands over the barn wood, peeked in the remaining window frames, and remembered the strangest things—like how Papaw liked to store random nuts and bolts in Mason jars, or how his tractor seat used to squeak—that I thought I'd long forgotten. And about the time that Alex and I were trying to decide if it was too muddy to walk up the hill to the chicken house, we rounded the corner by what used to be the carport, and I spotted something out of the corner of my eye that I never expected to see.

Let me explain.

When I was four or five, Mamaw and Papaw added a screened-in side porch off their kitchen. It ran the length of the carport and was pretty utilitarian: it had a three-quarter bath for Papaw to wash up after he'd been outside all day, a screen door that led to the backyard, another one that led to the carport, and a laundry room that housed Mamaw's washer, dryer, and deep freeze—along with all the vegetables and jellies and pickles she canned in the summertime.

(Mamaw's homemade plum jelly deserves its own chapter.)

(Just know that there's not a Thanksgiving that passes when I don't wish for some to put on top of my cornbread dressing.)

The screened-in porch burned to the ground during the fire, but the day we visited, the porch's cement slab was right where it had always been. I could even see where the pipes used to run into the bath. And off to the side of the spot where that bathroom used to be, Mamaw's cast iron kitchen sink was sitting right side up, as easily identifiable as it had been when I was a child.

Granted, it was considerably worse for the wear. Layers of rust and dirt covered the original porcelain coating; leaves and limbs filled the sink basin to overflowing. But there was no doubt that it was her sink, and the sight of it conjured all sorts of mental images: Mamaw moving back and forth between the sink and the stove, Mama and my aunt Chox washing dishes after Sunday lunch, Paige and me reaching up to twist the faucet handle so we could get a drink of that ice cold Moss Rose well water, Mamaw turning around and grinning at Papaw while he read the paper at the kitchen table.

And as Alex and I stood there and stared at that sink, as I tried to figure out how in the world that sink was still in one piece, as I realized that Alex was probably thinking, *Um, Mama, I don't get it—it's just an old, rusty sink,* one very clear and concrete thought began to form in my brain:

HOW DO I GET THIS SINK IN MY CAR?

Oh, and I wasn't one bit kidding, either. I wanted that sink in my car RIGHT THAT SECOND, and while I didn't really know how I was going to move it, much less carry it, much less load it, I WANTED THAT SINK. I wanted a tangible reminder of Mamaw's life, something that I could eventually use in my own kitchen as a daily reminder of how she loved and served her family. It didn't make a lick of logical sense, but in that moment, standing on that land, looking at all that grime and rust, I wanted that sink as much as I've ever wanted anything.

And with that deep want firmly established, I began to envision all sorts of take-the-sink scenarios. In fact, in the interest of adequately communicating my frame of mind, I will share a few of those scenarios at this juncture.

> Plan #1: Powered by a collective surge of superhuman strength, Alex and I would carry the sink to my car.
> Plan #2: I would use a giant chain to attach the sink to the back of my Highlander.
> Plan #3: I would walk to the nearest house and see if the homeowner had a small trailer I could hitch to the back of my car.

All of these options seemed totally feasible for approximately twenty-four seconds.

Eventually, though, I started to snap out of my hypothetical sink-stealing reverie, and when clarity settled in, here's what I knew for sure:

> Reality #1: I don't actually own a chain large enough or strong enough to attach a cast iron sink to a mid-size SUV.

Reality #2: Even if I could attach the sink to the Highlander, I'm pretty sure it would fulfill every single Mississippi stereotype to drag a sink down the interstate.

Reality #3: Dragging the sink via chain also comes with a high probability of SPARKS.

Reality #4: That sink probably weighs 150 pounds, and the only help I have in this south Mississippi pasture is a ten-year-old boy and an eighty-year-old woman. Picking up anything heavier than a brick is what we would call HIGHLY UNLIKELY.

Reality #5: Assuming Alex and I got the sink to the fence (under the influence of the aforementioned surge of superhuman strength), there's basically no hope at all for getting the sink over the fence unless Mama has secretly been powerlifting.

Reality #6: Pretty sure there's no trailer hitch on the back of the Highlander.

Reality #7: SNAP OUT OF IT, WOMAN—THIS SINK DOES NOT BELONG TO YOU, YOU'RE NOT TAKING IT ANYWHERE, AND P.S., YOU'RE ALREADY TRESPASSING.

So finally—completely resigned to my sink-less fate—I grabbed Alex's hand one more time, walked away from the sink, and headed in the direction of the car.

But I bet I turned and looked at that sink at least five times before we left.

I stopped just short of blowing a few kisses in its general direction.

If you've been paying really close attention up until this point, you know that so far two primary duos have served as the objects of our discussion and, clearly, our affection: (1) Mary and Elizabeth, and (2) Ruth and Naomi. With Mary and Elizabeth we broke down the implications of the verses in Luke 1 that cover their time together, and with Ruth and Naomi we looked at big ideas from each of the four chapters. Hopefully some of those takeaways will inform and affect the ways we interact with / minister to / take care of the women ahead of us and behind us. Hopefully revisiting their stories will encourage us to cheer on other women in Jesus' name. Because while there's no doubt that Mary, Elizabeth, Ruth, and Naomi had enormous influence as mothers, it's also good to remember that they also blessed the body of Christ as trailblazers for female friendship across generations.

Which leads us to Lois and Eunice.

And let's just go ahead and get this disclaimer out of the way: Lois and Eunice are mentioned in Scripture for, like, *a minute*. The only time we even see their names is in the first chapter of 2 Timothy, when Paul pointed out Timothy's spiritual heritage:

> I am reminded of your sincere faith, a faith that dwelt first in your grandmother Lois and your mother Eunice and now, I am sure, dwells in you as well. (v. 5)

There's at least one person who just read that last part and thought, *That's it? A SENTENCE? AND YOU NAMED YOUR BOOK AFTER ONE OF THEM?*

You'd better believe I did.

For a whole host of reasons.

But before we get into that, an anecdote.

A few years ago I heard Beth Moore teach a lesson on 2 Timothy 1, and she asked us to figure out if we were closer to Timothy, Eunice, or Lois in terms of our age. Since there was a pretty wide range of ages in attendance, she also told us that for the purposes of that particular afternoon, we'd consider the women between twenty and thirty-nine as the Timothys, the women between forty and fifty-nine as the Eunices, and the women sixty-and-up as the Loises. Having recently turned forty-one, I was clearly in the Eunice camp, and I happened to be with one of my very best friends, Melanie, who was two months shy of her fortieth birthday.

That means she was still thirty-nine.

Well, at the end of our lesson, we all stood up and spoke a blessing/commissioning over the women who belonged to different generations. The Timothys and Eunices blessed the Loises, the Timothys and Loises blessed the Eunices, and the Eunices and Loises blessed the Timothys.

That means that Melanie had to bless me as an older woman in her life, which was kind of funny, honestly. But when I had to bless her thirty-nine-years-and-ten-months-old self as a younger woman in my life? I may have struggled to find the humor in that specific moment.

Melanie, however, was as delighted as I've ever seen her. So maybe this is a good time to point out that sometimes, as we reach out to the generations behind us and ahead of us, we will be deeply humbled.

Or maybe even a little ticked off because CROSS ON OVER, SISTER; YOU ARE PRACTICALLY MY SAME AGE.

So yes. I'm a Eunice. Duly noted. And I say that not just because of the age ranges in the Bible lesson I mentioned, but also because by anyone's standards, I'm in the middle stage of my life. I'm a daughter and a wife and mama and most definitely not a young'un anymore—but I haven't crossed over into Lois territory just yet.

My Eunice-ness doesn't stop there. Because Eunice, as best we can tell from her lightning-fast appearance in Scripture, was a mama who was doing her best to pass along what she knew to her son. She was intentionally reaching out to the generation behind her and working (with her mom, Lois) to train up Timothy in the way he should go (Prov. 22:6). In 2 Timothy 3:14–15, Paul even reminded his younger friend to "continue in what you have learned and have firmly believed, knowing from whom you learned it and how from childhood you have been acquainted with the sacred writings, which are able to make you wise for salvation through faith in Christ Jesus."

In other words: "Your mama and grandmama have raised you right, Timothy."

As someone who, like Eunice, is also a mama, I pray that any teaching/training I've done with Alex will have that kind of impact. Granted, I know there have been times when I've probably passed on a little too much information about pop music and my favorite YouTube videos, but I sure do hope that David and I are giving our boy a foundation of faith that can withstand whatever the world throws his way. I know that he's *heard* our love for Jesus, but oh have mercy I pray that he's *seen* it, that he trusts it, and that as he continues to grow in his own faith, he'll have the courage to follow Jesus however and wherever He leads.

Because Lord willing, I cannot wait to see Alex Hudson become a man who consistently and joyfully walks in the truth (3 John 1:4). I know so many of y'all share that same desire for your sons, daughters, nieces, nephews, godchildren, next-door neighbors, coworkers, calculus students, Bible study girls, YOU NAME IT.

And here's the other part of that. While the whole notion of "spiritual children" isn't specifically addressed in 2 Timothy, I don't think it's much of a leap to say that Paul was building on the foundation that Lois and Eunice established for Timothy. Paul loved Timothy like a son, and certainly he took him under his spiritual wing. He even addressed Timothy as "my beloved child." So even though Timothy had a Greek biological father (Acts 16:1), he also had a spiritual father in his friend and mentor, Paul.

What a great reminder that when it comes to investing in the generation behind us, sharing our faith with them, leading them, and even serving with them, we're not limited to the folks in our immediate families. Titus 2:3–5 exhorts older women to "[teach] what is right and good, so that they may encourage the young women to tenderly love their husbands and their children, to be sensible, pure, makers of a home [where God is honored], good-natured, being subject to their own husbands, so that the word of God will not be dishonored" (AMP). That admonition applies whether we're related or not.

Bottom line: If you know people who are younger than you are? And you also know people who are older than you are? And you genuinely desire to love and serve those folks in Jesus' name? EUNICE AWAY, my friends.

Last thing.

Maybe the biggest reason I'm so drawn to Eunice and what she represents is because of two key words Paul used: "sincere faith." Paul said that Timothy's "sincere faith" was "a faith that dwelt first in your grandmother Lois and your mother Eunice." Maybe I'm overstating the obvious, but it seems to me that a sincere faith in Jesus is a faith with some impact. Sincere faith is genuine faith; it's not manufactured, it's not sugar-coated, it's not manipulative, it's not self-righteous, and it's not condemning. It's *real*—and it's faith we put into practice smack-dab in the middle of the good, the bad, the heartbreaking, and the joyful.

And when I think about the people who have had the biggest impact on my personal walk with the Lord, this is their kind of faith. Sincere faith is what I see in my parents. It's what I see in older friends like Mary Jo and Anne and Pattie and Marcia and Vickie and Pat and others who have made the time to speak into and over my life. It's what I pray the younger people in my life see in me.

Don't get me wrong. I'm a work in progress FOR SURE. But what I know beyond a shadow of a doubt is that there is no greater adventure than surrendering to the abundant life we have in Jesus. I would have never believed it when I was twenty-two, but embracing the purpose God has entrusted to us for our good and His glory? Following hard after the One who is the same yesterday, today, and forever?

It is the biggest blast you and I will ever have.

Paul knew it. I can't help but think that Lois, Eunice, and Timothy knew it, too.

And if you know it?

Don't hide that light under a bushel, sister.

Pass it on.

So. About that sink.

I really didn't take it that day we visited Moss Rose.

But I've been thinking about it for three years.

And I know it's still in the same spot, primarily because Paige and her family went down to Mamaw and Papaw's old land for their own walk-around a couple of months ago. Paige also had a tearful reunion with the sink and the slab and the chimney cleanout door as she stood there in the middle of the pasture, and she probably would have pitched a tent and spent the night if not for that pesky trespassing business.

Well.

For the last few months David and I have been talking about updating our kitchen, which is currently stuck in all manner of 1988 glory. I don't know when we'll finally get around to starting the project—there are about sixteen things ahead of it on our house to-do list—but I have already vowed and sworn and declared that if there is any possible way to make it happen, my new kitchen sink will be Mamaw's old one. Legally acquired, for sure. Refurbished and restored, of course.

And yes, if you think about it, going to Lowe's or Home Depot would be so much easier. We could pick out a new sink in fifteen minutes and probably have it installed within a couple of days. On a scale of zero to total hassle, a brand-new sink registers way lower on the annoyance meter.

Mamaw's sink, though, means something to me. It was an integral part of how she cared for our family, how she demonstrated her love, how she taught us, and how she showed us who she was. I'm pretty sure I learned everything I ever knew about Mamaw while I was sitting in her kitchen. That sink is worth the trouble.

But all that being said, here's what occurs to me.

If I am that committed to a seventy-five-year-old sink—if it carries such significance in my life that I am willing to (very foolishly) contemplate ATTACHING IT TO MY VEHICLE WITH A CHAIN—then how much more should I be fighting for the stuff that *really and truly matters*? Yes, I have a strange attachment to that old piece of cast iron, but at the end of the day, it's just a thing. It symbolizes something, but it's not the something.

Because what I miss about Mamaw Davis isn't her sink. It isn't her kitchen. I do miss her apple tarts a whole lot, for sure—and if you'd ever had them, you would, too—but they're certainly not biggest part of this deal.

So here's what I really miss.

I miss her wisdom. Her calm. Her humility. Her gentleness. And while I know it was faith that brought those qualities to life in her, I would give anything to be able to talk to her about it. I'd give anything to be able to grab her hand and look in her eyes and say, "I see Jesus all over you. How did that happen? How does your faith impact your marriage? How did it shape the way you raised your babies? When do you feel closest to the Lord? What do you love the most about Him?"

I have so many questions for her, y'all.

And that sink will never be able to answer them.

It's weird, isn't it? In so many ways we get fixated on what we're going to leave people when we die or what they're going to leave us when they do. Family members claim certain pieces of furniture, argue over who is going to get the silver, and threaten to write off their siblings if they don't get Aunt Gertrude's crystal water goblets. We can get ridiculous about the dumbest things; we act like an antique bed or a sterling platter or an Oriental vase is the very essence of the person who passed away.

And listen. As someone who clearly has a vested interest in an old cast iron sink, I understand why those things can be special.

But in the end, it's all just stuff.

And stuff will never, ever be the same thing as legacy.

So in these last couple of chapters, we're going to look at the big picture of why all of this matters—whether we're a young'un, a middle-aged 'un, or an older 'un. We're going to dig into a couple of questions that I hope will get to the heart of why cross-generational relationships are so important in the here and now.

What have we inherited?

What are we passing on?

Because that "sincere faith" that "first dwelt" in Lois and Eunice?

THAT IS THE TICKET, Y'ALL.

That's what we ought to be fighting to haul out of people's pastures, so to speak.

So if you'll permit me, I'm going to err on the side of personal and reflective in this last section. I want to talk about how the sincere faith of other women—my mama, in particular—has impacted my own walk with the Lord. And I want to tell you where my heart is in terms of caring for the next generation.

Come to think of it, you might want to warm up a little bit before you keep reading. Swing your arms back and forth. Do a few shoulder rolls. Because ultimately—hopefully—we're going to lift our arms, open our hands, and get ready to reach out to the women on either side of us.

It may require some stretching, but the good news is we'll be more limber than ever.

And who knows? I might finally be able to pick up that sink.

(I can't help it. I still want it.)

(I'm only human, after all.)

Chapter 12

The Sweetest Legacy

In the photograph I'm thinking about, I was around two years old, sitting on the den sofa in the house where I grew up, dressed for bed in a long-sleeved white T-shirt with matching footie pajama bottoms. The sofa upholstery was a blue and green patchwork pattern with so much going on that even Carol Brady might have taken a look at it and said, "Hey, Sims family—I think you could probably tone down the color palette a few notches." But as the picture clearly shows, that crazy '70s sofa was the perfect contrast to the blonde wood paneling behind it, and if the pattern was too busy, I certainly didn't seem to mind. My favorite toy, a wooden clock, was resting against my right leg, but I'd fixed my attention on what was going on to my left. That's where Mama, dressed in her satin housecoat, was singing a made-up song as she carefully combed through the curls in my favorite doll's hair.

Mama wasn't wearing any makeup; if I had to guess, she'd probably cleaned her face with Merle Norman cleansing cream and then followed up with Merle Norman Aqua-Lube moisturizer.

(Back then Mama wouldn't dream of using anything other than Merle Norman products; she was adamant that everything else aggravated her sensitive skin.) She'd bobby-pinned sections of her copper-colored hair in order to prevent an epic case of bedhead the next morning; Mama might not be high-maintenance in many areas, but like so many Southern women, she has always been meticulous about her hair.

What stands out most to me in that picture, though, is something most people probably wouldn't see—something I know way down deep in my bones, something that I know my sister and my brother would see in that picture, too.

When she was with her children, Mama had all the time in the world.

No matter what Mama was doing with us when we were little, she was unrushed, unhurried, and uninterested in doing anything other than being right where we were. Family was always her biggest priority, and we knew it. Looking back, in fact, I recognize that there was a whole lot she *didn't* do so that she could be home with us; she never served on a bunch of committees or went on girls' trips or jumped on board with the latest mom-trends. She just liked to be home.

And that didn't change when we three kids (sort of like "We Three Kings," only not at all like that) started to get a little older.

Since I'm the youngest in our family by ten years, I was the only child at home by the time I was seven, and if I didn't know it before, my elementary school years taught me how happy it made Mama to have all her people under one roof. If Sister planned to come home for a weekend, Mama would dust and fluff the house for days beforehand, changing sheets and turning back beds and cleaning windows. Then she'd spend a full afternoon steaming broccoli for Chicken Divan, cooking peas, frying okra, making squash casserole—whatever she thought would make Sister the happiest. If Brother happened to be on a break from college, Mama would go to Burnett's Grocery and ask the butcher to cut up five or six chicken fryers. Then she'd spend the rest of the day moving pots and skillets from the stove to the oven and back again so that come suppertime, she could serve a Southern feast: fried chicken, rice and gravy, butter beans, fresh tomatoes, corn, and pound cake.

When I left for college the pattern continued; my meal of choice for weekends at home was always Mexican cornbread or anything that prominently featured potatoes, oh hallelujah. And for holidays or special occasions that brought all the children—which, by my junior high years, included Sister's husband, Barry—home at the same time, Mama would TURN IT OUT with the hospitality: gallons (seriously, gallons) of her homemade chicken salad, more fresh vegetables than you could shake a stick at, the most delicious, perfectly seasoned turkey breast east of the Mississippi, creamed potato casserole (can I get an amen?), beef tenderloin, homemade rolls, you name it.

And all that food set the stage for what seemed like nonstop conversation. Mama always wanted to hear what our friends were up to, and she loved to catch us up on the latest hometown news. Daddy and the rest of the men in the family would usually move to the den to watch a game or pass around the newspaper, but the women would sit in the room off of Mama's kitchen for hours, swapping stories and drinking coffee and occasionally even scratching each other's backs (it's a thing in my family—we are all like a pack of cats in that regard). It might just be Mama, Sister, and me, or it might be the three of us plus an assortment of aunts and cousins and friends. But regardless of numbers, Mama was her happiest and most content when she was at home with her people. *She had all the time in the world for us.*

And I think it's safe to say that no matter how old we got, we never left Mama and Daddy's house feeling hungry.

It was certainly true for our stomachs. But it was also true for our souls.

As Brother, Sister, and I grew up—the finish-college-get-jobs-buy-homes-settle-down-kind of growing up—Mama, who is mostly known as "Mama Ouida" in my hometown—continued to pour her life into ours. She loved to visit us in Memphis and Nashville and Baton Rouge, loved to help us decorate, loved to cook for us, loved to visit with us. And then, after Brother married Janie and grandbabies entered the picture, Mama loved to rock those baby boys, loved to swaddle them after their baths, loved to cook them pancakes and make them chocolate pies and scratch their backs for two or ten or ninety-four minutes.

(I really wasn't joking about the back scratching.)

(PACK-O-CATS.)

After David and I moved to Birmingham and Alex came along a few years later, Mama would stay at our house for a week at a time, usually, and it proved to me once and for all that serving her family was the great joy of her life. She loved nothing more than tackling every bit of our laundry over the course of a day (I

210

have long contended that by Mama's standards, one towel totally qualifies as a full load), hanging out with Alex, shopping with me at Home Goods and Stein Mart, making up beds so they looked like something at the Four Seasons, and tending to the ferns on our front porch with as much care as she would show her family. She has always loved to make things beautiful, and there was something about the way she folded towels and organized cabinets and rearranged picture frames that brought order and peace into what sometimes resembled chaos. I would beg her to rest, to take it easy, to let us wait on her, and she always had the same response: she'd grin, point her finger, and say, "Sophie? Hush. This is what I love to do. Let me do it."

So we did.

About four years ago, though, something shifted. It was subtle, and really, at first, it was a just a general impression of the tiniest, slightest distance. Ever since I was in college, Mama and I talked two or three times a week—even if a phone call only lasted a few minutes—and the result was a two-decades-long running conversation about, well, pretty much everything. Somewhere around Mama's eightieth birthday, though, the phone calls started to diminish in frequency. Sometimes Mama wouldn't call for a week or two, and when I'd call her, she'd uncharacteristically cut our conversations short; she'd say she wasn't feeling well, she didn't have any news, she was cleaning out closets (this excuse was actually the most feasible, because Mama derives more joy from a well-functioning closet than could probably be considered normal). Over and over I'd remind myself that she was eighty and perfectly entitled to talk or not talk as little or as much as she wanted, and Sister would often add the perspective that sometimes it gets difficult for older people to carry on phone conversations. None of that, however, changed the fact that I missed her. And since I knew she was physically healthy—save a few aches and pains common to the twilight years, of course—I found myself frustrated by the fact that she didn't seem to want to spend as much time with all of us.

It was just—I don't know—*weird*.

Later that same year Mama and Daddy came to our house for the week of Thanksgiving, and the only way I know to explain the general vibe of that visit is that Mama didn't want to talk. She wasn't rude at all—she wouldn't dream of that—but for the first time ever, she didn't want to sit down and have a conversation. She wanted to organize Alex's closet and clean out his toys and sweep the deck and vacuum the rugs. And while I know y'all probably think it's strange for me to be talking about an eighty-year-old woman who WOULD NOT SIT DOWN, you have to consider that my parents have always been incredibly active. Daddy pretty much does all the same things he did at fifty-five (with the exception of officiating football and basketball games—though he still loves to run a game clock), and Mama's eightieth birthday hadn't tempered her ability to GET AFTER IT. She was slower, absolutely, but her commitment to the task at hand was the same as it had always been.

What I missed, I guess, was the balance she'd always had. I missed how she'd drink coffee and thumb through a *Southern Living* magazine while she chatted about how she'd like to decorate her front porch. I missed hearing her imitate family members' voices when she'd tell stories. I missed the sound of her laugh. I wanted her to sit down and talk like she'd always done, but she wasn't having it, and after a couple of days, I decided she must be mad at me. I wondered if she thought I made a mistake going back to work full-time, if I hurt her feelings in some way, or if my inability to keep up with laundry had finally driven her to the brink of frustration. None of that made any logical sense to me, but the change in her disposition was like a puzzle I couldn't solve.

After three or four days of watching Mama focus nonstop on chores, the distance was driving me crazy (which was the craziest thing considering that she was right here in my house). My hope was that we could have a conversation about whatever was going on, so I walked down the hall to Alex's room, which was the last place I'd seen her. I will never forget that I found her in Alex's closet, moving plastic bins of hand-me-downs from one side to the other, and as gently as I knew how, I said, "Mama, please stop. Seriously. Please stop working. We want to spend *time* with you. You've been doing stuff like this ever since you got here, and in addition to the fact that we don't want to see you work like this, we miss you."

At that point I could tell that I was about to cry, but I choked back the tears because EASY ON THE DRAMA, GLADYS.

And here's the part I will never forget.

Mama looked at me, smiled half-heartedly, and sighed. Then she said, "Well, I don't know what to say. But I'm so happy cleaning. And really, I guess I'm just not much of a conversationalist."

It was the oddest response, I thought. And considering that Mama had been holding court at our family gatherings for most of my life, it wasn't even the tiniest bit true.

Clearly, though, she believed it.

She turned around and walked back in the closet.

And that was that.

On Labor Day of last year, Mama and Daddy came to our house for a long weekend (Martha, too! Martha was here! She was just so happy to be here!), and as we normally do, we planned a big day-o-shopping for Saturday. For most of my life Mama has been on a perpetual hunt for "a good, black knit top"—you can never have enough, I reckon—and Martha's ever-evolving like-to-find list (I believe I mentioned it a few chapters ago) ensures that she always has something to look for. So Saturday morning, after everybody was up and dressed and ready to go, Mama, Martha, and I set off for the first stop on our shopping adventure: Nordstrom Rack.

As soon as we got to the store, Mama and I walked over to look at a rack of skirts while Martha headed in the direction of some jackets (IMAGINE THAT). I was hoping to find a few things to wear to work, so I pointed toward a section of blouses and told Mama that I was going to look there for a few minutes. Eventually I put a couple that I liked into my shopping cart before I turned and asked Mama if she wanted to look at shoes, but she shook her head.

"I'll just stay here," she said.

It was maybe ten minutes later—after I'd tried on about four pairs of booties along with a wedge or three—when I started to wonder what Mama was doing. I pushed my cart out of the shoe section and into the back aisle of the store, doing my best to look over the racks in the hopes of spotting Mama's light silver hair. I walked the perimeter of the store without seeing her, and as

I started my second loop, I realized that a vague panic was settling over me. It was a feeling similar to a few years before when I walked outside to call Alex in for supper and he was nowhere to be found. It turned out that he was playing next door, thank goodness, but for the two or three minutes when I couldn't find him, my legs felt like they were made of Jell-O.

My reaction in Nordstrom Rack wasn't quite that extreme, but still, I was concerned. When I reached the front of the store for the second time, I looked outside—which, in retrospect, was a strange choice—but for some reason I was scared that Mama had wandered off. I kept having flashbacks to my Uncle Joe and his Alzheimer's and one time when he got disoriented in a restaurant, so I told myself that I'd make one more loop, and if I didn't see her, I was going to call Daddy and David for help. I couldn't call Mama—because she doesn't have a cell phone.

I KNOW.

By the time I started my third loop, I was worried out of my mind, though I couldn't put my finger on why. After all, we've shopped together and gotten separated and found each other hundreds of times over the course of my life. But this was different. I couldn't have told you how, exactly, but I knew that it was. And I kept looking.

At the end of my third loop, I had started to reach for my phone when I spotted her. She was sitting in a chair at the front of the store, and I tried to control my voice as I ran up to her.

"Mama? Mama! Where have you been? Mama! I've been looking for you everywhere!"

And y'all, there was something about the way she looked at me that stopped me in my tracks. It only lasted a split-second—just a tiny sliver of time—but I knew she was confused. I still don't know exactly what happened; maybe she was scared, maybe she reached back in her mind for my name and couldn't find it, maybe she couldn't figure out why I was running up to her in a strange store. Regardless of why, it was clear that something about that whole situation was a mystery to her. It was about thirty seconds before her face relaxed, and when it did, she smiled.

So I asked her the question again.

"Mama? Where have you been? I've been looking for you everywhere!"

After a long pause, she answered me very slowly:

"Well. I'm right here."

And she was.

She was right there.

And that was all that mattered.

The following Christmas, as Sister has said so many times since, was a humdinger.

In November and December, we'd had several conversations with Daddy about Mama's health, mostly wondering what was going on and what would be the best way to help her. Eventually we decided that a head-to-toe physical was in order, so we made her a doctor's appointment for mid-January. Mama was still as kind and loving as she'd ever been, but she was even more reserved and quiet than she'd been that time when I tried to talk to her in Alex's room. Plus, when she and Daddy came to our house for Thanksgiving, they planned to spend the weekend with us but only stayed one night. Mama said she was ready to go home, and we didn't argue with her. Somehow we could tell that home was what she needed.

Christmas, however, made us hopeful. With the exception of Thanksgiving, Mama began to embrace a new pattern when she'd visit. As I cooked or cleaned up or moved clothes from the washer to the dryer, she'd settle in a chair right off the kitchen, wrap up in a blanket, look at magazines, drink a glass of tea, or—no kidding—she'd re-read my first book. I never asked her why she read it so often, but one night, when I walked past her bedroom and she was sitting up in bed, reading the book again, I stopped, poked my head in the door, and said, "Mama? Aren't you sick of it yet?"

She grinned and said, "No. I'm not." That sweet response actually nagged at me, mainly because I'd noticed that Mama's sentences were getting shorter. I told David several times that Mama seemed to answer questions in as few words as possible, which meant we heard a lot of cheerful yeses and nos in her distinctive Mississippi drawl. Sister and I tried to remind each other that given Mama's age, things weren't going to be the same as they'd always been, but there was no denying the change in her speech pattern.

And it bothered us.

Mama and Daddy had been in Memphis at Brother and Janie's house for several days before Christmas, so they drove to our house on Christmas Day. And I realize that right now there are probably several of you who are thinking, *What in the world? Why are your eighty-something parents on the road on Christmas?* Well, that's because it's HOW MY DADDY LIKES IT. He is an eighty-four-year-old man in a fifty-five-year-old body, and he's basically up for a road trip on any given day of the week—provided he can play eighteen holes of golf and then walk four miles before he loads the car and hits the road. He's remarkable.

Within an hour of their arrival, Sister and I knew that something was off. Mama seemed nervous—frantic, almost—and after she went into the guest room and shut the door for probably the fourth time, Sister followed her. I was in the kitchen, trying to finish cooking supper, so I couldn't hear what they were saying. But about a half hour later, Sister walked into the kitchen.

"What in the world is going on?" I asked. "Is Mama okay?"

Sister tried to fight back tears, but it was no use.

"Mama said"—Sister took a deep breath—"that she's having a hard time 'following through.' She said that she gets started on something—like cooking breakfast or balancing her checkbook or maybe just asking a question—and she can't remember how to finish. She can't follow through."

There was nothing else to say, really. So we just stood there, Sister and me, crying the saddest, quietest tears as Christmas carols played over the kitchen speaker.

Granted, no one had officially diagnosed what was going on with Mama, but in that moment, both of us knew.

Somehow, on some level, we knew.

It was a dreary January day when I drove to my hometown to take Mama to her doctor's appointment. I arrived at Mama and Daddy's house late that Thursday morning, and the first thing I noticed was that Mama was rattled. She hadn't put on her makeup, she wasn't dressed to the nines (as is her typical preference), and she couldn't find the earrings she wanted to wear. I tried to lighten the mood by reminding her that we were just going to the doctor's office, so she didn't need to be bejeweled and bedazzled, but Mama wasn't amused. She was annoyed, honestly, and my steady stream of lighthearted chitchat wasn't helping matters. I made a mental note to ZIP IT, grabbed Mama's fire engine-red purse, and helped her out to the car.

We made it to her appointment on time, and after a couple of hours of evaluation, the doctor decided that Mama needed to be hospitalized. There were some numbers and some vitals and some whathaveyous that gave the doctor pause, and she wanted to run a few tests to try to pinpoint what was going on. Mama was also in need of some significant medication tweaks, and the hospital was the best place to do that what with the abundance of trained medical personnel.

(Unsolicited Public Service Announcement: when people get older and they see a lot of doctors, everybody might not know what everyone else is prescribing, not to mention that some older patients might get dosages mixed up. Those mixed-up dosages can result in a medical condition that I have come to refer to as DANGER, WILL ROBINSON, DANGER.)

(Seriously, adult children of elderly parents. We have to make our parents' medications our business.)

(Also: I'm glad we had this talk.)

Mama was none too pleased about going in the hospital, but I kept reminding her that she was going to get some rest, she was going to get her blood pressure down from OH, DEAR GUSSIE levels, and she might even get a definitive answer about why, in her words, "I can't talk anymore."

After I filled out the 429 forms required for admission (thanks, America!), an orderly took us to Mama's hospital room. It was essentially a shoebox with one corner cut out for the restroom, and while I didn't have an official thermostat anywhere on my person, my best educated guess—primarily based on the heat blast that singed my eyebrows when we first opened the door—was that the cozy shoebox's temperature was roughly 85 degrees.

Okay. Maybe that's an exaggeration. It was probably 82 degrees. Clearly I should have taken a wool coat.

Mama spent most of Thursday afternoon and Friday morning being wheeled away for different tests and scans; her doctor wanted the specialists who were on call to have all the information they needed. But even with all those tests going on, Mama made incredible progress within the first forty-eight hours: her blood pressure came down, her hydration levels went up, and her dosages were adjusted so that her medications would work better together. She was more alert, more rested, and much more like her old self.

But we still didn't have a diagnosis.

Saturday morning Daddy and I were sitting with Mama when the neurologist stopped by. Mama was eating breakfast, trying to coax some flavor out of the hospital grits, so she wasn't paying a whole lot of attention to what the doctor was saying. I looked sideways at Daddy when the neurologist mentioned the same condition another doctor had suggested as a possible diagnosis the day before, and because I am a person who requires significant overexplaining, I wanted to ask him about it. I asked if I could talk to him in the hall.

Mama was still giving those grits her full attention when the doctor and I walked out of the room.

"So," I began, "I'm just curious if I heard you correctly a few minutes ago. You were talking about Mama's test results—did I hear you say that she has dementia?"

"Yes. I did say that," he answered.

"Because Dr. H mentioned it yesterday, but I wasn't sure if it was the final diagnosis, or if there was something else . . ."

"No, it's dementia," he said, matter-of-factly. "Mild to moderate. We can tell based on the brain scan."

I should have been ready with eight or nine deeply thoughtful follow-up questions. But I was trying to process what I was hearing, trying to make it sink in my head and my heart, and I could only think of one more thing to ask.

"So. She doesn't need to drive, does she?"

"Um, no." He laughed the tiniest bit. "Definitely not. No driving. But we'll start her on some medicine that will slow the progression of the disease, and really, given her age, this isn't an unusual condition."

So that was it.

On one hand, it was heartbreaking news. It was both what we had suspected and also what we had feared.

On the other hand, though, it was an answer. It explained so much: the withdrawal, the speech problems, the trouble "following through." It was almost like finding the missing pieces to the puzzle of the past few years. And even though I absolutely, one hundred percent bawled my eyes out when I took a break from hospital duty to take a shower at Mama and Daddy's house—even though I would cry right now if we were talking about this in person—I felt so grateful for that answer.

Finally, we knew.

We really knew.

And since we knew, we could deal with it.

So Daddy and I talked, and he was as sweet as he could be, and I may have repeated the part about MAMA CAN'T DRIVE at least four times. We spent the rest of the afternoon hanging out in that glorified closet, Daddy and I both fully aware that the road ahead was going to look very different than the road behind us. But I'll tell you this (and really, I can only tell you this because I'm typing; if we were talking, I'd never get past some impressively prolific sobbing): the way my daddy responded to Mama and her diagnosis is something I believe will ripple in our family for generations. No kidding. Every time I thought of a new way their lives were going to change, Daddy had it covered. He would do the cooking, he said. He could dust and run the vacuum. He could change the sheets, he said, and he didn't mind taking Mama to her hair and nail appointments, either. He'd do the grocery shopping, no problem. He'd manage her medication. We'll handle it just fine, he said.

(And now that a year has passed? I can say without hesitation that he has done every bit of that—and so much more. He takes the best care of his bride of sixty-two years, and I can't talk about it anymore or I'll have to get in the bed and will never finish writing this book.)

(I'm sure you understand.)

So Saturday, it wasn't necessarily the happiest day. But Saturday night, I looked over at Mama and realized that her eyes were sparkling again. She wanted to sit up, she wanted to watch TV, she wanted to laugh, and she wanted to FIX HER HAIR, glory to God. So I washed her hair, got her back in the bed, set up her gigantic magnifying mirror, and handed her a bag full of Velcro rollers. Mama didn't do much talking, but she smiled. Oh, did she ever smile. I even snapped a picture of her as she rolled her hair; she looked like she was forty years old and getting ready to go somewhere fun with Daddy. It was like someone had taken all the internal uncertainty and worry and confusion of the last three or four years and lifted it right off of her.

I remember thinking that she looked like someone who had been seen.

Really, truly, deeply seen.

And the reason I know what that feels like?

She taught me.

I'm pretty sure that if Mama was having a really good day with her words and you asked her what she taught her children—especially what she has passed on to her girls—she'd say, "Oh, just a few practical things. Probably not all that much." And if you asked her if she tried to follow Lois's and Eunice's lead in terms of passing on "sincere faith," she'd say that she did her best, but she certainly wouldn't dream of comparing herself to women in, you know, *the Bible.*

I would beg to differ.

Mama taught us that the first will be last, and the last will be first. She taught us to trust the Lord in every circumstance, to remember "all things work for good, for those who are called according to his purpose" (Rom. 8:28).

She taught us to go ahead and spend the extra dollar to buy Land-O-Lakes butter, to always make sure pound cake ingredients are at room temperature, and to fry okra in small batches so that the corn meal doesn't clump.

She taught us that people are made in the image of God; therefore, they are precious—each and every one. She taught us to listen to that "still, small voice," and that if someone keeps coming to mind and you have no idea why, you'd probably do well to stop and pray for that person. She taught us to worship.

She taught us how to do a lot with a little, how to make a pot of coffee, and how to set a killer table. She taught us the secret to Mamaw's cornbread dressing recipe, the wonder of a sweet potato casserole, and the blessing of a fresh tomato. She taught us that a good meal brings people together, but a bad meal makes everybody sort of ornery.

She taught us to make good meals.

She taught us how to welcome, how to love, how to comfort, and how to care. She taught us to get the log out of our own eye, to forgive, and to move on. She taught us that love covers a multitude of hurts, and sometimes, when you don't necessarily feel very loving, sticking with someone out of pure stubbornness will do just fine.

She taught us that the Lord cares about the smallest details of our lives, that we can and should talk to Him about anything, and that we can trust Him no matter what.

We can trust Him.

No matter what.

So now, in this bittersweet phase of our family's life, when the tables have turned and our sweet mama needs us more than ever, I think I can speak for Sister and Brother when I say this:

We have all the time in the world for her.

As much as she needs. As much as it takes.

She's the one who taught us that, you know.

And she still has so much to teach us.

That's a very good thing.

Because we still have so much to learn.

Chapter 13

May the Circle Be Unbroken

So sometimes, if I'm waiting for Alex to finish practice or maybe just looking for a way to kill a few minutes before an appointment, I like to look at the comments on people's Instagram pictures.

What? You thought I was going to say that I like to explore exegetical fallacies in Scripture? Or I like to contemplate modern-day pitfalls in eschatology?

Oh. I am terribly sorry. I mean, I understand this is the final chapter of this book and all, but I guess now is as good a time as any to very gently let you know that if that was your expectation, you may have confused me with someone else.

Because give me a small-ish window of spare time, and BRING ON THE INSTAGRAM. Sure, the pictures are great, and I get a huge kick out of being able to keep up with what's going on in people's lives. But as someone who spends a considerable amount of time working with teenage girls, I can tell you without hesitation that Instagram comments are a goldmine if you're looking for some insight into the lives of young women in their late teens / early twenties.

Let me explain.

When I was in high school and college, we wrote notes to our friends. We wrote letters. We created sentences and paragraphs and lo, even the occasional novella so that we could (1) explain our feelings to our friends, (2) encourage and affirm our friends, (3) communicate what was going on in our lives with a degree of detail and clarity that phone calls didn't always allow—especially if you had a sibling who kept picking up the receiver in the other room because he/she really needed to make a phone call, too.

(Can y'all even believe that we used to have to SHARE PHONES with people?)

(Obviously I grew up in the Stone Age.)

Now I don't know about anybody else, but all those words coming from people who loved me were absolutely life-giving. I knew that my people were for me because they made a point to write it down and tell me. Sure, we still had the negative voices in our heads and, to a much smaller degree than girls face now, we had some pressure from media to be beautiful and charming and whatnot. But more often than not, affirmation came from real-live people who took the time to put words to paper and build up instead of tearing down. So by and large, when older women spoke over us and into our lives, most of us tended to believe and trust them. Typically we didn't have any reason not to.

And that brings us back to Instagram comments. Or any social media, really. Take your pick. Only I'm not picking Snapchat because it seems like a lot of selfies and I feel like it would get on my nerves.

No judgment if that's your fave, though. Free country, etc.

So in the interest of finally making a point, here's a random sampling of comments that I've seen on my younger friends' Instagram pictures.

Prepare to behold some serious depth.

Here we go.

I will number them to make this collection seem somewhat more official.

1. Total babes
2. Hotties
3. yessssss
4. Love
5. hbd
6. ily
7. Fire
8. Ok
9. Hotties!!
10. Omg you're perfect
11. Hair goals
12. outfit >
13. literally perf
14. baaaaaaabes
15. ily a mily
16. Hawt
17. omg tiny
18. TINY
19. Bae
20. u look guuuuud

I think that'll do.

And obviously, OF COURSE, I'm picking and choosing. There were some very sweet comments in the mix, along with a pretty good assortment of snarky ones. But here's my big, fat point:

All of those comments might make somebody feel better for, like, four seconds, but there's not a whole lot of substance there. Granted, I grew up during a time when the emphasis was "pretty is as pretty does"—my friends and I felt not one iota of pressure to be sexy or hot or "hawt," for that matter—but wouldn't it be great if we could back off the obsession with how people look for just a minute?

If we could type out a whole sentence of encouragement?

Or if we could double-tap the picture instead of reducing photographs to a public commentary about someone's appearance?

Does anybody else think that this is a weird way to interact with people?

It's not that I'm opposed to telling younger girls that they look beautiful or that their hair is pretty or that I like their dress. But our younger generation is already under enormous pressure to look a certain way, and I think that when lots of girls are essentially training each other to strive for "baaaaaaabes" and "omg tiny" and "Hotties!!" then they're setting each other up to settle for superficial.

IT MAKES ME CRAZY.

But here's what I have to remind myself: there is GOOD NEWS in the middle of all of this.

It doesn't have to be this way.

Because do you know what we see in Mary, Elizabeth, Naomi, Ruth, Lois, and Eunice? We see some substance. We see some wisdom. We see some blessing. We see some intention. We see some care.

And every bit of it was for the good of those women and the glory of God.

I don't know about y'all, but I want those things so desperately for the generation behind us. They deserve so much better than what the culture is saying to them. And I keep thinking that if Lois and Eunice were in the business of passing along "sincere faith," then that's a pretty good goal for all of us present-day Loises and Eunices as well.

By the way, that doesn't mean that we have to go big and publish a "Sincere Faith" Bible study and put up some fliers at Starbucks before we start planning our first "Sincere Faith!" event, launching in fall 2018.

It just means that we look around at the places where we've earned a voice in someone's life. Maybe it's a daughter. Maybe it's a coworker. Maybe it's a couple of cousins. Maybe it's a neighbor.

That's a lot of maybes, right? But those maybes are a really good thing—because they remind us that the relational possibilities are wide open.

So here's the challenge: wherever you have influence with the generation behind you, start investing. Pray that the Lord will help you find the folks He'd like for you to encourage.

He's "literally perf" at that sort of thing, you know.

Now before I talk for a few minutes about the older women in our lives, I would just like to be clear and say if there's a trend on Instagram where our sixty-plus friends are calling each other "bae," I am blissfully unaware.

In fact, I went to my friend Mary Jo's Instagram to see what's going on in her comments, and mostly she and her friend Jane are talking about greenery and orchids. This is enormously encouraging to me, because when I'm in my seventies (Lord willing), I pray I'll be just as focused on how to make things grow and thrive.

I may have just amen'd myself.

And really, I may have also (unintentionally) summed up why it's so important for us to have older women in our lives: *they know what makes things grow.*

They know how to grow plants, sure, but they also know how to grow in faith, how to grow in marriage, how to grow in singleness, how to grow in friendship, how to grow in parenting, how to grow in a relationship with the Lord. And in addition to all that growing, they know how to establish roots that are deep and well-nourished, they know how to prune away what's no longer necessary, and they know what it takes to bear fruit.

Which reminds me of something.

A few months ago I spoke at a church in Birmingham, and because of the way the event—which is an annual Christmas show house—is organized, I spoke four times in two days. I got to hang out with some folks I don't get to see nearly enough, and after the last session on the second night, I stayed way later than I probably needed to because I was having so much fun.

Around 8:30 I started to convince myself that it was time to go home. As I was gathering all my stuff from the table where I'd set it down, a woman, probably in her mid-seventies introduced herself. She immediately told me that she had volunteered for both days of the event, so she listened to me give the same talk four times.

This elicited no small amount of sympathy from me.

Anyway, we were talking about this and that and the other thing, and as she was telling me a little bit about herself and her husband, she mentioned that for many years she was the primary caretaker when her mama was suffering from dementia.

Now I was listening before she said anything about dementia, but *after* she said it? I was LOCKED IN. I hadn't mentioned anything about Mama's health when I was speaking, so that sweet lady had no way of knowing what we're dealing with in our family. But considering that just a couple weeks before I'd spent several days at Mama and Daddy's to help while Mama recovered from foot surgery, there was so much about Mama's condition that was fresh on my mind. There were parts of it that I hadn't quite figured out how to process; and even though yes, this is our "new normal," it's still *new.* There's so much we still don't know.

My new friend and I stood in the back of the Fellowship Hall and talked for thirty or forty-five minutes. I felt like I could be completely candid with her because I knew she understood, and I wouldn't take anything for the sweetness of that conversation and the comfort of her words. The Holy Spirit united our hearts almost instantly, and after we finished talking and said our good-byes, I felt like I'd been to church.

So it may surprise you to know that I haven't talked to her since.

And there's a very good reason why I want to make sure you know that.

Sometimes we can get bogged down in thinking that we need a mentor and we have to find a mentor and why can't we find a mentor because, clearly, ALL THE MENTORS ARE TAKEN.

And they're not, of course. But while you're waiting or looking or praying, making a point to incline your ear to the older women around you. Seriously. Take advantage of opportunities to have a conversation. Listen to your aunts interact with each other at your next family get-together. Take doughnuts to a Sunday school class full of seventy-somethings at your church. Make a hair appointment for 10:00 on a Friday morning and soak up the stories as women settle in for their weekly wash and set.

Maybe I'm oversimplifying, but you certainly don't need a mentor to build relationships with older women. I mean, if there's a down side to putting yourself in a position to honor and listen to women of faith who have so much to teach and so much to share, I can't think of it. Unless you easily tire of older women telling you how young and cute and darlin' you are. But that would pretty much be the only potential drawback.

And who knows? In those conversations you may find that you click with someone, or you may realize—like I did at the Christmas event—that the Lord wants you to hear from someone who has been right where you are.

So here's the challenge: wherever you have interaction with the generation ahead of you, start blessing. Pray that the Lord will help you find the folks He'd like to come alongside you.

And in the company of those good growers? I bet you'll bloom like crazy—no matter where you're planted.

I mentioned a couple of chapters ago that Lois and Eunice are only in Scripture for a tiny period of time. And really, when Paul acknowledges them, it's almost in the form of a shout-out. It's like he's standing at a podium, building up Timothy with his words, and when he gets to the part about Timothy's grandmother and mother, he pounds his chest twice and then blows a kiss. Lois and Eunice certainly aren't main characters in Paul's narrative, but because the Word of God is deep and rich and trustworthy and true, we can actually extract some significant takeaways from their brief appearance in the book of 2 Timothy.

So. Would you like to hear more about that?

Oh, I'm so glad.

Look! I made you another list!

1. **You can't underestimate the impact of women working together for the good of the generation behind them.** I realize that Timothy breaks the pattern of our women-taking-care-of-women concept, but the big idea is the same. Lois and Eunice joined forces across their generational lines so that they could serve the young whippersnapper who was coming up behind them. They taught him the "sacred writings" of the Old Testament, and then, when Paul came into the picture, he built on that foundation and led Timothy to saving faith in Christ. Lois's and Eunice's teaching, investment, and care empowered Timothy to walk out his calling. Their faithful discipleship prepared

him to follow the Lord, to serve people, and to impact the nations. Thumbs up, Lois and Eunice.

2. **We can't offer people support if we're not receiving support ourselves.** The Lois/Eunice combo reminds me that if we're going to pour ourselves out relationally, we have to be filled up. HAVE. TO. BE. Spending time with the Lord is critical, of course, and so is community. Knowing that Lois and Eunice served together makes me wonder if there were times when they were getting ready to teach the sacred writings and Eunice said, "Mama? I CANNOT EVEN. Not today. Can you handle the lesson this morning?" Knowing that someone can be strong when you're weak is such a comfort. Plus, knowing that someone has your back makes all the difference. When we're not operating in a healthy, supportive relational environment, dynamics get warped, relationships get codependent, and people get hurt. It stands to reason that Lois and Eunice supported one another in an honoring way; pettiness, drama, and competition don't breed "sincere faith."

3. **Lord willing, your obedience will ripple in ways you never know or see.** Maybe this is a Captain Obvious moment, but in addition to cheering on other women in their callings, your intention in cross-generational relationship gives you the opportunity to share the gospel and see the Lord's saving grace transform lives. Paul's words remind us of that. He said that the sincere faith that dwelt first in Lois and Eunice now dwells in Timothy—and that Timothy needed to "fan into flame the gift of God" that he received when he trusted in Christ for salvation. Then,

in 2 Timothy 4:2, Paul told Timothy to "preach the word; be ready in season and out of season; reprove, rebuke, and exhort, with complete patience and teaching." Timothy the student had become Timothy the teacher, and his "sincere faith" no doubt impacted others for the cause of Christ just as his grandmother's and mother's did him. And you know what that makes me wonder? How many people eventually came to know Jesus as result of Lois's and Eunice's faithfulness? I would sit and try to work up a hypothesis with that, but math.

4. **You have to be a student before you can be a teacher (or a follower before a leader) (or however you'd like to phrase it).** There have been so many times in my life when I've wanted to teach lessons that I hadn't learned yet, when I wanted to pass along some nugget-o-truth that hadn't even begun to take up residence in my head or my heart. When we're trying to teach what we don't really know, we're putting ourselves in a place where our voice may have some volume but it will not carry a lick of authority. We're marching straight into clanging cymbal territory. Lois and Eunice were effective in training up the generation behind them because they knew what they were teaching backward and forward. Just like Elizabeth did with Mary and Naomi did with Ruth, Lois and Eunice were passing on what they had learned way down deep in their souls. So from that perspective, I think, we can't ever stop learning and growing deeper in our faith—because those two things are critical components of our teaching. We don't just want to be smart; we want to be wise. Proverbs 4:7

says, "The beginning of wisdom is this: Get wisdom, and whatever you get, get insight." Before we teach or pass on anything, we should be people who pursue wisdom; we should "Pray for [wisdom], take pains for it, give diligence in the use of all appointed means to attain it . . . get it *above all thy getting.*"[33]

5. **Plant the seeds and trust that the Lord will bring the harvest.** So, in this current era of momagers—mamas who like to map out a plan and then work out some details on behalf of their families—it's tempting (especially for those of us in the Eunice crowd) to think that we can strategize and program and plan A Meaningful Discipleship Experience (with Proven Results!). But here's what Lois and Eunice did: they faithfully scattered seed. We don't have any reason to think that they micromanaged, that they orchestrated Timothy's first meeting with Paul so he could network and make connections, that they walked up to Paul and offered him a very detailed testimonial about all the ways that Timothy was so very gifted. *They scattered seed.* However that played out was up to the Lord. This is so good to remember when we find ourselves building relationships with older or younger women; it's not our responsibility to fix everything so that it looks pretty (and listen—I *so* get this since I am a fixer by nature). Because ultimately, the last thing we want is a makeover; we want substance and wholeness and impact. Only God can do that.

Good talk, team.

Some of you have probably been reading all my words about honor and wisdom and investing in the generation behind us and thinking, *This is all very easy for you to say, ma'am, because in case you didn't notice, you work with teenage girls for a living. You have no choice but to invest in their lives. THEY HAVE YOU SURROUNDED.*

Yes. Yes, indeed. These are very fair points.

But I can tell you for a fact that I'd be hopeless with those girls if not for women who are a step or two ahead of me, women who have taught and led and loved me so selflessly. They've come in all forms, too: family members, teachers, coworkers, Bible study leaders. They know better than anyone what a reluctant learner I've been at times. But they've stuck with me and stuck by me and let me see what real faith looks like in the context of real life.

They have been the sweetest gifts.

Well.

A few days ago I ran in the grocery store because I realized that I had approximately zero items to put in Alex's lunch for the next day—unless, of course, he wanted to enjoy a questionable can of cream of celery soup along with some stale Veggie Straws.

It just so happened that I was right on the brink of my personal emotional precipice as I wheeled up and down the aisles; I had just returned home after a funeral for my friend Daphne's mom, so my mind was full of thoughts about Barbara's influence and love and kindness in our lives. Plus, she and Daph were unusually close— a couple of like-minded, like-hearted women—and it made my heart hurt to think about Daph having to endure the loss of her sweet, smart, funny mama. Even now it breaks my heart to think about the text Daph sent me after her mama passed away: "She was the best person I knew."

So my heart was full and my eyes were teary as I blazed through the Publix, and I was just about to grab a loaf of bread off the shelf when I saw Martha (not my mother-in-law! Not that one! This is a different Martha!), a friend who taught math for many years at the school where I work. Different Martha retired about ten years ago and could quite possibly be the twenty-first-century prototype for the quintessential Southern grandmother. She is a nurturer through-and-through, and while she has daughters of her own, she has also been a faithful mentor to younger women in her church.

Different Martha asked me about school, and I asked about her granddaughter who graduated from high school last year, and we traded stories for about five minutes when she asked me how the book stuff was going. I caught her up on the progress of the book you're reading right now—told her that I hoped to be turning it in within the week—and she said, "Oh! That's so exciting! What's it about?"

And I said, "Well, it's about cross-generational friendship—how younger women need older women and older women need younger women. How we're meant to walk through life together."

It wasn't my most, um, *articulate* explanation. But Different Martha was totally tracking with me. She smiled, nodded her head, offered all sorts of encouragement. And then, after she paused for a few seconds, she said, "You know what? That's how I've always tried to live my life."

"I know you have," I replied. "I've watched you do it."

So we said our good-byes, and I moved on to the cheese aisle (who's surprised?), but after I bought my groceries and walked out to the car and put everything in the trunk, I sat down in the driver's seat, put my head in my hands, and cried like a baby.

Because Different Martha, she went straight to the heart of things. I could have quoted her on page one and typed "The End" right after I closed the quotations.

This whole cross-generational thing isn't a program. It isn't a fad or a trend or a member multiplication tool. It's real life. And like Different Martha, I believe it's how we're supposed to live our lives: blessing and learning from the ones ahead of us, investing in the ones behind.

I'm so grateful for Mary, Elizabeth, Naomi, Ruth, Lois, and Eunice—six women in Scripture who took care of their people in the most personal, life-giving, God-honoring ways. Six women who show us how to honor, how to persevere, how to cling, how to glean, how to partner, and how to pass it on.

No strategies. No methods. No checklists.

Just wide-open hearts, an abundance of tender, loving care, and a one great, big, awesome God who faithfully provides us with the perfect people at the perfect time. Sometimes it's because we need to learn, sometimes it's because we need to teach, sometimes it's because we need to bless, and sometimes it's because we need to heal.

And in and through every bit of it, we can look around at the women who surround us and echo Mary's words: ". . . for he who is mighty has done great things for me, and holy is his name" (Luke 1:49).

Get out there, girls. And get after it.

Giddy up.

notes

1. See http://thevillagechurch.net/resources/sermons/detail/freedom-in-the-fight.

2. Ibid.

3. See http://www.desiringgod.org/messages/love-one-another-with-brotherly-affection.

4. Ibid.

5. See https://www.blueletterbible.org/Comm/baxter_mary/WitW/WitW29_Elizabeth.cfm?a=974041.

6. See https://www.biblegateway.com/resources/matthew-henry/Luke.1.39-Luke.1.56.

7. See https://www.blueletterbible.org/Comm/baxter_mary/WitW/WitW29_Elizabeth.cfm?a=974041.

8. Ibid.

9. See https://twitter.com/bentgreene/status/523530237989371905.

10. See https://twitter.com/bethmoorelpm/status/520201206070005760.

11. See http://www.theatlantic.com/national/archive/2014/03/here-is-when-each-generation-begins-and-ends-according-to-facts/359589.

12. See https://www.barna.org/barna-update/millennials/711-what-millennials-want-when-they-visit-church#.ViQ0shCrTVp.

13. Ibid.

14. See https://www.barna.org/barna-update/culture/722-five-factors-changing-women-s-relationship-with-churches#.ViQ1fhCrTVo.

15. See https://www.blueletterbible.org/Comm/baxter_mary/WitW/WitW29_Elizabeth.cfm?a=974045.

16. See http://www.jesuswalk.com/lessons/1_39-56.htm.

17. See https://www.biblegateway.com/resources/matthew-henry/Luke.1.39-Luke.1.56.

18. See https://www.blueletterbible.org/Comm/guzik_david/StudyGuide_Rth/Rth_1.cfm?a=23300.

19. Herbert Lockyer, *All the Women of the Bible* (Grand Rapids, MI: Zondervan, 1988), 117.

20. Ibid.

21. See https://www.biblegateway.com/resources/matthew-henry/Ruth.1.6-Ruth.1.18.

22. See http://www.enduringword.com/commentaries/0802.htm.

23. See http://www.convert-me.com/en/convert/volume/bibephah.html.

24. See https://www.blueletterbible.org/Comm/baxter_mary/WitW/WitW16_NaomiAndRuth2.cfm.

25. See http://www.hymnary.org/text/in_the_harvest_field_now_ripened.

26. *The MacArthur Study Bible* (Nashville, TN: Thomas Nelson, 2013), Ruth 2:20 footnotes.

27. See https://www.blueletterbible.org/Comm/mhc/Rth/Rth_003.cfm?a=235001.

28. "Please Be Patient with Me" by Wilco.

29. See https://www.biblegateway.com/resources/matthew-henry/Ruth.3.14-Ruth.3.18.

30. See https://www.blueletterbible.org/Comm/guzik_david/Study Guide_Rth/Rth_4.cfm?a=23600.

31. See http://www.radical.net/files/uploads/LoveStory_TS4_Web. pdf.

32. *The MacArthur Study Bible*, 364.

33. See https://www.biblegateway.com/resources/matthew-henry/ Prov.4.1-Prov.4.13.

Acknowledgments

My deepest thanks and so much gratitude to:

Lisa Jackson, Jennifer Lyell, Heather Nunn, and the B&H Publishing team, Melanie Shankle, Heather Mays, Liz Shults, Shawn Brower, David Balik, Laura Thompson, Jean Castille, Perry Griffin, Bobby Wilkes, the BCA small group, and my Briarwood girls.

My GAP girls—Amelia, Ann Kelly, Emily, Genie, JuJu, Katherine, Kathryn, Mary Glynn, Molly, Rachel, and Shelly—as well as my forever friends and my unbelievably supportive family.

And most of all:

Alex—Your love for people makes me want to love people better. Having a front-row seat for your life is such a blast, and I get the biggest kick out of seeing the Lord shape and mold you into the young man He's calling you to be. Also, you are hilarious. This is a huge plus in our family. And your laugh is my favorite sound on the planet.

David—You work so hard for us and take such good care of us. You are steady and strong and the best decision-maker I know. You support all this writing stuff unconditionally, and that is no small feat. Thank you for reading every word before anybody else. And thanks for laughing with me every single day.

I love y'all.

So if there is any encouragement in Christ, any comfort from love, any participation in the Spirit, any affection and sympathy, complete my joy by being of the same mind, having the same love, being in full accord and of one mind. Do nothing from selfish ambition or conceit, but in humility count others more significant than yourselves. Let each of you look not only to his own interests, but also to the interests of others. (Phil. 2:1–4)

About the Author

Sophie Hudson loves to laugh more than just about anything. She began writing her blog, BooMama.net, in November 2005, and much to her surprise, she's stuck with it. Through her stories, Sophie hopes that women find encouragement, hope, and laughter in the everyday, joy-filled moments of life. A devoted fan of pajama pants, Sophie loves cheering like crazy at college football games and watching entire seasons of TV shows in record time. She lives with her husband and son in Birmingham, Alabama.

Connect with her in the following places:

Blog: BooMama.net

Facebook: www.facebook.com/SophieHudsonBooMama

Twitter: @boomama

Instagram: boomama205